SHORTCUT 3

365 LEADERSHIP QUOTES

by LINKED IN AND TOWN HALL ACHIEVER OF THE YEAR
EY NOMINEE ENTREPRENEUR OF THE YEAR
GRAND HOMAGE LYS DIVERSITY
WORLD TOP100 DOCTORS

Dr BAK NGUYEN, DMD

TO ALL THOSE LOOKING TO WALK THEIR LEGEND AND TO MAKE THE WORLD A BETTER PLACE.

by Dr BAK NGUYEN

ISBN:: 978-1-989536-76-6

Published by: Dr. BAK PUBLISHING COMPANY
Dr.BAK 0095

DISCLAIMER

« The general information, opinions and advice contained in this medium and/or the books, audiobooks, podcasts and publications on Dr. Bak Nguyen's (legal name Dr. Ba Khoa Nguyen) website or social media (hereinafter the "Opinions") present general information on various topics. The Opinions are intended for informational purposes only.

No information contained in the Opinions is a substitute for an expert, consultation, advice, diagnosis or professional treatment. No information contained in the Opinions is a substitute for professional advice and should not be construed as consultation or advice.

Nothing in the Opinions should be construed as professional advice related to the practice of dentistry, medical advice or any other form of advice, including legal or financial advice, professional opinion, care or diagnosis, but strictly as general information. All information from the Opinions is for informational purposes only.

Any user who disagrees with the terms of this Disclaimer should immediately cease using or referring to the Opinions. Any action by the user in connection with the information contained in the Opinions is solely at the user's discretion.

The general information contained in the Opinions is provided "as is" and without warranty of any kind, either expressed or implied. Dr. Bak Nguyen (legal name Dr. Ba Khoa Nguyen) makes every effort to ensure that the information is complete and accurate. However, there is no guarantee that the general information contained in the Opinions is always available, truthful, complete, up-to-date or relevant.

The Opinions expressed by Dr. Bak Nguyen (legal name Dr. Ba Khoa Nguyen) are personal and expressed in his own name and do not reflect the opinions of his companies, partners and other affiliates.

Dr. Bak Nguyen (legal name Dr. Ba Khoa Nguyen) also disclaims any responsibility for the content of any hyperlinks included in the Opinions.

Always seek the advice of your expert advisors, physicians or other qualified professionals with any questions you may have regarding your condition. Never disregard professional advice or delay in seeking it because of something you have read, seen or heard in the Opinions. »

ABOUT THE AUTHOR

From Canada, **Dr. BAK NGUYEN**, Nominee Ernst and Young Entrepreneur of the year, Grand Homage Lys DIVERSITY, LinkedIn & TownHall Achiever of the year and TOP 100 Doctors 2021. Dr Bak is a cosmetic dentist, CEO and founder of Mdex & Co. His company is revolutionizing the dental field. Speaker and motivator, he wrote 72 books over 36 months accumulating many world records (to be officialized). His books are covering:

- **ENTREPRENEURSHIP**
- **LEADERSHIP**
- **QUEST OF IDENTITY**
- **DENTISTRY AND MEDICINE**
- **PARENTING**
- **CHILDREN'S BOOKS**
- **PHILOSOPHY**

In 2003, he founded Mdex, a dental company upon which in 2018, he launched the most ambitious private endeavour to reform the dental industry, Canada wide. Philosopher, he has close to his heart the quest of happiness of the people surrounding him, patients and colleagues alike. In 2020, he launched an International collaborative initiative named **THE ALPHAS** to share knowledge and for Entrepreneurs and Doctors to thrive through the Greatest Pandemic and Economic depression of our time.

In 2016, he co-found with Tranie Vo, Emotive World Incorporated, a tech research company to use technology to empower happiness and sharing. U.A.X. the ultimate audio experience is the landmark project on which the team is advancing, utilizing the technics of the movie industry and the advancement in ARTIFICIAL INTELLIGENCE to save the book industry and to upgrade the continuing education space.

These projects have allowed Dr Nguyen to attract interests from the international and diplomatic community and he is now the centre of a global discussion in the wellbeing and the future of the health profession. It is in that matter that he shares his thoughts and encourages the health community to share their own stories.

"It's not worth it go through it alone! Together, we stand, alone, we fall."

Motivational speaker and serial entrepreneur, philosopher and author, from his own words, Dr Nguyen describes himself as a dentist by circumstances, an entrepreneur by nature and a communicator by passion.

He also holds recognitions from the Canadian Parliament and the Canadian Senate.

SHORTCUT 3

365 LEADERSHIP QUOTES

by Dr BAK NGUYEN

INTRODUCTION

by Dr. BAK NGUYEN

Here I stand, once more, at the beginning of a new journey, starting my 95th book, **Shortcut volume 3, Leadership**, hours after Apple Books and Amazon distributed the first 2 volumes internationally.

By now, it is a matter of hours between the submission of my script and its availability in the world, even in paperback form. I don't know if there is a world record for that, but it surely speaks volume.

It is official, I am entering my last month before the dateline of August 31st, to complete my challenge of setting the next world record of writing 100 books within 4 years. 31 days, that is not much to go with. Including this one, I still have 6 books to write before reaching 100.

But wait, even with my effort, **COVIDCONOMICS** and **CRYPTOCONOMY** will not be ready on time. **COVIDCONOMICS**, even if I spent the last week pushing the project travelling the country, still have to wait for the events to unfold.

And **CRYPTOCONOMY**, when I started the project, the pace and timeline of the crypto market were aligned with mine... and then, everything went down the drain. Since the journey is to take 50K to a million and to share the story, I am nowhere near having something to report except for my losses and the interview of Martin D. Weiss, the only authority quoting that space.

In short, I will have to make up for these 2 books. That's a total of 8 books to write within the next 31 days. That's a little less than 4 days per book. Last year was crazy and I had 8 days per book... is this even possible?

I must admit that I feel the fatigue and lack of motivation at my doorsteps. The last week travelling the country and not writing also gave me some perspective... Whatever you think, think again!

Well, I started last week in Vancouver, looking to travel as far as possible within the Canadian borders to avoid any restrictions and confinement rules about COVID. I also needed to cover that part of the country for the writing of **COVIDCONOMICS**.

Well, on my first morning in Vancouver, I had an international meeting between Canada, the USA, and Spain. Long story short, I was introduced to an American veteran producer, who is interested to take **THE ALPHASHOW** to Netflix, Amazon Prime, and the other big media outlets. Let me repeat that. I am finally making my way to Hollywood!!!

20 years ago, I failed at the door of Hollywood, embracing my dental licence instead of risking it all. 20 years later, I have a new opening. I will not miss this one.

As the day went by, I finally realized what was really happening to me: I always wanted to be a producer and filmmaker, that's a behind-the-camera role; now, I am the face in front of the camera, anchoring the **ALPHAS**! Never in my wildest dreams, I would have seen myself as an anchor, my face on Netflix and PRIME! I guess that this is the **POWER OF YES**!

That gave me a big boost in morale as I pushed the following days to shoot the videos for **COVIDCONOMICS**. I went all in! That also left me with literally no time for writing, none!

And here I found myself, in the final countdown of my 4th year with 8 titles to write. It is now about motivation and stamina. On that, I was fortunate that as I was looking for inspiration and motivation, the 2020 Tokyo Olympics were starting.

I changed my habits of writing listening to movie soundtracks to having the Olympics playing in the back. Watching the women swimmers pushing themselves and one another to break new heights and new heights, I finished the compilation of **SHORTCUT volume 2** within 3 days, between checking out from the Vancouver Fairmont, the trip back to Montreal, and the jetlag.

I wrote following the vibe. Well, if you listen to the introduction of the athletes, with world records, national records, multiple olympian, medalists, best qualifying time, you got buried under the announcements and the introductions. And then, the race starts and within minutes, it all unfolds to first, second and third place.

"Literally, everything that was so intimidating
a minute ago was old news fading in the back."
Dr. Bak Nguyen

That's quote #2432 and that's life in the fast lane! These athletes trained for years and years. Whatever they've accomplished is just good for their introduction. What really matters is their performance of the day and nothing else. And then, some will shake it off, medals and deceptions, to concentrate on their next competition, following within the next hours... that's the Olympics!

I stand in admiration of such spirit and force of character: to stay light, to be ready, to give it our best, and to move on. This is what I got from watching the Olympics:

"Humility and determination are the trade of Olympians, the athletes."
Dr. Bak Nguyen

Here is quote #2433. So enough with the introduction. In **Shortcut volume 1** - we uncovered our demons, got rid of our denials, and started our **HEALING** process. Then, in volume 2, we picked up the pieces and started rebuilding, from the ground up, our own persona and identity. It was all about **GROWTH**.

Well, this is the 3rd chapter of the series, and **RISING** is next. But RISING is the title of my 62nd book. This is on top of the fact that rising is much too large to be contained in one volume.

So I made an executive decision and we will go right to the point. If I shared as much with you, it was to inspire and empower you to find your powers and to walk your destiny. Well, we all know what comes with powers… responsibilities. I also told you times and times over that growth happens at the giving end; and that to last and to avoid resistance, it should always be about the others first.

Following that line of logic, what is **RISING**? What kind of rise am I preparing you for? You should know me well enough by now: to make the world a better place! And so, the third volume of **SHORTCUT** and the first under the theme of **RSING** is **LEADERSHIP**, to make the world a better place for all of us!

Within this journey, it will all be about gaining influence, boosting your persona and narrative, and yes, leading others to greatness.

LEADERSHIP will be divided into 4 categories of quotes: 163 Leadership quotes, 89 Society and Diversity quotes, 42 Alpha quotes and we will end will these famous 77 Dr. Bak's quotes.

From Influence and vision to putting them to good use in Society, in harmony. Then, the Alpha quotes will reinforce the leader and the driver in each of you.

"If HEALING takes time and GROWING is painful,
RISING is the best part!"
Dr. Bak Nguyen

Here is quote #2434. And here it is, your rise to your legend. This is **Shortcut volume 3, LEADERSHIP**. Welcome to the Alphas.

If I have changed the world from a dentist chair,
you are all in a better position to change the world than I am.
Dr. BAK NGUYEN

PART 1

"LEADERSHIP"

by Dr. BAK NGUYEN

What is leadership, other than the obvious? To most, to too many, leadership is about control and giving orders. If that's your idea of leadership, you were born in the wrong era.

Power is about control and giving orders when applied in the most common form. I will unveil myself completely in this chapter. I hate control. Above anything, there is nothing that I hate more than someone telling me what to do, even worst, what to think and how to feel about it.

Yes, I was raised in a very strict immigrant family. I spent all of my childhood going to church every Sunday morning. I complied and asked questions. People were only interested in the compliance, not in the questioning part. The answers were either BS, have faith or you will understand one day.

They could have mold out of me a great general, instead, all they did was to push me to seek my answers elsewhere. By they, I meant Conformity, Education, my parents, even culture.

Instead, I found my answer in between the lines of History. History, not as teachers like to teach it, but in books and movies, reading the fact and the in-between the lines.

Much younger, I excelled in History class. Most of the teachers and of my peer students thought that it was because that I have a great memory. Not quite. History is mainly the story of conquests, wars, and peace treaties.

What I read and heard walking back History was to put myself in the shoes of those in command. The rest was simply logic and consequences unravelled.

"Follow the money."

That is usually the logic of detectives and inspectors as they are trying to solve crimes and mysteries. Well, I did the same, I followed the *money*. Money in terms of power, money in terms of greed, money in terms of lust, money in terms of jealousy.

Do that and look at History, you will see a very familiar story repeating from one era to the next, only the names and the ***props*** differ.

I read History from the Antiquity, from the Roman Empire, The Hans Dynasty, The French Kingdom and then, as it became an empire, The rise of the American empire, and

Greek mythology and Hebrew history (Bible) in between, I must say that the themes are the same, always coming back.

It took me a few years further down the road, as I started to be compelled to take an active role in Society and leadership, I started to apply what I learnt from History, only, this time forward, always *following the money* and putting myself in the shoes of those making the decision. Suddenly, I discover the power to read the Future with a certain accuracy.

"History taught me a way to read the Future."
Dr. Bak Nguyen

That's quote #2435. As I was called to put my name forward to run for office, I could see the faces of everyone I read in my childhood. From Caesar to Napoleon to the Cardinal de Richelieu to Phoebus (Notre-Dame de Paris) to Agamemnon, the faces and inside stories were all too familiar to me... And the worse narratives are of those that History never remembers their names... well, these narratives are the ones that repeat themselves the most often.

I saw the truth and I did not want to fight my way through that crowd. Instead, I found my refuge in playing music and dreaming of a better world. I said dreaming, actually, it was creating new paths where I saw a specific angle and where I felt a possible victory… with minimum resistance.

I was often right. I was also wrong more than once. But always looking for the path with least resistance, I elevated myself and grew my influence without fights, without troupes, without war nor casualties.

Most people don't even know that I exist, but those who know my name are those with the power to make a difference. From them, I earned respect.

Was that leadership? Never would I say yes, until I heard the exact words coming out of their mouth.

"Leadership attracts leadership."
Christian Trudeau

That was coming from one of my mentors and friend, a man who created billions for the number 1 telecommunication company of Canada, a man whose name is from the dynasty of our political system, a man whose past is my hope of future. I could not deny the facts any longer.

Then, I got invited to visit the United Nations Secretary of Africa, I got proposals to host private banquets for prime ministers, I got the attention of people looking to make a difference. I became influential.

"Influence is power without liability."
Dr. Bak Nguyen

Even in the dental community, a community in which I keep my distance, I was amazed by the influence that I hold within the COVID war.

"Power is not about friendship. Power is about one.
Power is about balance and counter-balance.
Well, I chose influence instead."
Dr. Bak Nguyen

That's the 2436th quote. But please, do not confuse power with leadership. Those in power love to call themselves leaders and to take over a leadership role.

Well, if it takes leadership to yield power, I can also tell you that not all of those in power have leadership.

Leadership is to have a vision and to unify other people around that vision in order to make it a reality. Power is the control over the crowd that gathered. As leadership is about making a difference, power is about controlling the difference.

Power is about management while leadership is about moving forward, about building. I am not making many friends writing these lines, but I kept quiet for much too long.

I am writing these words as I am a doctor in dentistry and hold no official position. And yet, I am more and more influential. How did I do that? By serving and empowering others.

No, these are not vain and empty words, I invite you to go through my books and writing, with close to 100 books and 2 million words written, there is nowhere for me to hide. I grew outside of the radars and with lesser resistance because I chose Influence over Power because I empowered instead of Ordering around.

That's how I managed to attract so many great minds to my table. Each of these people is of the caliber of my mentor and master. Yet, none of them consider themselves as such, they are happy to share their friendship.

"To make a difference for others,
that is the key of Influence."
Dr. Bak Nguyen

And that is quote #2437. You don't have to believe me, I co-wrote books with some of these great minds, I invite you to find these books and to read what was said of me. Usually, if one is lucky, he or she might have the privilege to have one mentor, maybe two, and never all at once. Well, my kind of leadership allowed me to have mentors talking to each other.

Because I chose **INFLUENCE** over **POWER**, I also avoid most of the liabilities coming with **POWER**. With less resistance, I grew my **CONFIDENCE** and grew secured enough to let go of exclusivity, of possessing, of one. My midlife crisis taught me much on the ***matter of one***.

What I did locally with great mentors, I repeated Internationally in the COVID war with **ALPHAS** from all around the world. I extended a welcoming hand to exchange and collaborate. I empowered each of the ALPHAS who came to me, I also empowered the audience as, in my mind, they were all Alphas too.

"To empower was my key to influence."
Dr. Bak Nguyen

And that is quote #2438. The danger is to know who you are empowering. Well, that's a danger within a danger as who has to judge the other person and his or her motive. Well, I said that in a quote that I keep close to my heart: "Every time that you are judging, you are chipping a little piece of your soul."

It took me 18 months of cure, saying YES to everything (**THE POWER OF YES** series) to get rid of that nasty habit of judging. So no, no judgment nor trial. Instead, I took the time to carefully go through my sharing, thoughts, and teaching to understand the core of its power.

Because the power taught is based on compassion and flexibility, one will need his or her heart at the right place to yield the secrets and powers that I am sharing with you.

But once your heart is in harmony with these vibes, pillars of the universe, the powers available to you are from another dimension.

If I started this chapter with the question of what is leadership, I will not impose my opinion. Instead, I will simply share with you my journey and see if that is of any appeal to you. If yes, you might find much wisdom and power in the journey ahead. If not, I will still be here when you are ready.

This is my leadership, a kind and friendly hand extended to you with the hope that you will do more and better than me, for the betterment of our future and world.

This is **Shortcut volume 3, LEADERSHIP**. Welcome to the Alphas.

PART 2

"163 LEADERSHIP QUOTES"

by Dr. BAK NGUYEN

0491

FROM SYMPHONY OF SKILLS

"The only thing that counts is what you've done."

Dr. Bak Nguyen

0492

FROM SYMPHONY OF SKILLS

"I don't care who is right, as long one of us is!"

Dr. Bak Nguyen

0493

FROM SYMPHONY OF SKILLS

"Doing good is not enough,
making a difference lasts, that's the only goal!"

Dr. Bak Nguyen

0494

FROM SYMPHONY OF SKILLS

"There are no perfect plans."

Dr. Bak Nguyen

0495

FROM SYMPHONY OF SKILLS

"Build on top of what is given."

Dr. Bak Nguyen

0496

FROM SYMPHONY OF SKILLS

"Entrepreneurs build and destroy,
be mindful of what is what."

Dr. Bak Nguyen

0497

FROM SYMPHONY OF SKILLS

"Do not confuse a thinker and an entrepreneur."

Dr. Bak Nguyen

0498

FROM SYMPHONY OF SKILLS

"We can move forward by fear or by ambition.
If we hesitate, the choice will not always
be ours to make."

Dr. Bak Nguyen

0499

FROM LEADERSHIP, PANDORA'S BOX

"The glory is not to sit on the top,
but to move the average up."

Dr. Bak Nguyen

0500

FROM LEADERSHIP, PANDORA'S BOX

"The greatness of our world is the compounded greatness of every single one of us."

Dr. Bak Nguyen

0501

FROM LEADERSHIP, PANDORA'S BOX

" A lionheart does not divide; it multiplies."

Dr. Bak Nguyen

0502

FROM LEADERSHIP, PANDORA'S BOX

" To matter means nothing unless it is to matter to others!"

Dr. Bak Nguyen

0503

FROM LEADERSHIP, PANDORA'S BOX

" Greatness is not in the size of the numbers, but the audacity of the reach."

Dr. Bak Nguyen

0504

FROM AMONGST THE ALPHAS, VOLUME 1

"To empower is not to give power but to help discover the power that each has within."

Dr. Bak Nguyen

0505

FROM LEADERSHIP, PANDORA'S BOX

"In all the legends, the best sword against a hero is his or her own. Don't fall under yours, your Pride."

Dr. Bak Nguyen

0506

FROM LEADERSHIP, PANDORA'S BOX

"Compounded Wills, not averaged Wills."

Dr. Bak Nguyen

0507

FROM LEADERSHIP, PANDORA'S BOX

"For as long as our hearts lead the day,
our mind and intelligence will ease the way."

Dr. Bak Nguyen

0508

FROM IDENTITY, ANTHOLOGY OF QUESTS

"To make a difference, one has to bear
more than his own weight."

Dr. Bak Nguyen

0509

FROM IDENTITY, ANTHOLOGY OF QUESTS

"Trapping synergy is not possible, you have to seduce
a synergy to keep it glowing and growing
into a momentum!"

Dr. Bak Nguyen

0510

FROM IDENTITY, ANTHOLOGY OF QUESTS

"Two is the natural state,
but it starts with two ones adding up."

Dr. Bak Nguyen

0511

FROM IDENTITY, ANTHOLOGY OF QUESTS

"The white gloves are off,
this is the war to hypocrisy!"

Dr. Bak Nguyen

0512

FROM IDENTITY, ANTHOLOGY OF QUESTS

"Averaging hides both the pride of the leaders and the fear of the contenders."

Dr. Bak Nguyen

0513

FROM IDENTITY, ANTHOLOGY OF QUESTS

"To have a vision is to draw the horizon on which the sun will eventually set and rise."

Dr. Bak Nguyen

0514

FROM PROFESSION HEALTH

"Plan from the top down and build from the ground up!"

Dr. Bak Nguyen

0515

FROM PROFESSION HEALTH

"Be humble but not naive, be strong but not stubborn."

Dr. Bak Nguyen

0516

FROM PROFESSION HEALTH

"Nothing can stand in the way of
a momentum of good, of synergy."

Dr. Bak Nguyen

0517

FROM PROFESSION HEALTH

"Nothing great is worth doing alone."

Dr. Bak Nguyen

0518

FROM PROFESSION HEALTH

"Alone, we will stand, but often not for long."

Dr. Bak Nguyen

0519

FROM INDUSTRIES' DISRUPTORS

"Alone, there's just so much we can do."

Dr. Bak Nguyen

0520

FROM INDUSTRIES' DISRUPTORS

"To refuse to bow down to the average is both
arrogance and humility at the same time."

Dr. Bak Nguyen

0521

FROM INDUSTRIES' DISRUPTORS

"No is just the first door to pass through."

Dr. Bak Nguyen

0522

FROM INDUSTRIES' DISRUPTORS

"Some risks are worth the fall they represent, some are just not worth considering."

Dr. Bak Nguyen

0523

FROM INDUSTRIES' DISRUPTORS

"You cannot reach new heights thinking of balancing... you may only succeed through excess and stubbornness."

Dr. Bak Nguyen

0524

FROM INDUSTRIES' DISRUPTORS

"Entrepreneurship is a way of life."

Dr. Bak Nguyen

0525

FROM INDUSTRIES' DISRUPTORS

"For as long that the alternative is to do nothing, I do with what I have in hand."

Dr. Bak Nguyen

0526

FROM INDUSTRIES' DISRUPTORS

"The best trait of an entrepreneur is his or her curiosity to never accept that it is over, that it is perfect, that it is completed!"

Dr. Bak Nguyen

0527

FROM INDUSTRIES' DISRUPTORS

"At its core, the entrepreneur is that kid who never gave up his or her curiosity and hope."

Dr. Bak Nguyen

0528

FROM CHANGING THE WORLD FROM A DENTAL CHAIR

" It's not worth it to go through it alone, and success tastes better alongside each other; but at the end of the day, it's always up to you to make it happen."

Dr. Bak Nguyen

0529

FROM CHANGING THE WORLD FROM A DENTAL CHAIR

" Leadership is mainly driven by the head while entrepreneurship has, at its core, the heart. "

Dr. Bak Nguyen

0530

FROM CHANGING THE WORLD FROM A DENTAL CHAIR

" Before, they called me crazy.
Today, they are eager to know more!"

Dr. Bak Nguyen

0531

FROM CHANGING THE WORLD FROM A DENTAL CHAIR

" The louder they scream, the scarier they are."

Dr. Bak Nguyen

0532

FROM CHANGING THE WORLD FROM A DENTAL CHAIR

"I don't wait either, no momentum was ever born from waiting."

Dr. Bak Nguyen

0533

FROM CHANGING THE WORLD FROM A DENTAL CHAIR

" Not always being the number one has its share of good and lightness! "

Dr. Bak Nguyen

0534

FROM CHANGING THE WORLD FROM A DENTAL CHAIR

" Connections instead of comparisons. That's the key."

Dr. Bak Nguyen

0535

FROM THE POWER BEHIND THE ALPHA

"Worth is gained as we are useful to others... stop self-serving just ourselves."

Dr. Bak Nguyen

0536

FROM THE POWER BEHIND THE ALPHA

"Ignoring the needs of the others
is the root of most evil. Ignorance."

Dr. Bak Nguyen

0537

FROM THE POWER BEHIND THE ALPHA

"They both also shared the attribute of being women of few words, very few words."

Dr. Bak Nguyen

0538

FROM MOMENTUM TRANSFER

"You show up to enjoy while you own to serve."

Dr. Bak Nguyen

0539

FROM MOMENTUM TRANSFER

"Embrace the day and make the most out of it! Make it happen! "

Dr. Bak Nguyen

0540

FROM HYBRID

"The day your name becomes a common expression, that day you've become one with your worth."

Dr. Bak Nguyen

0541

FROM HYBRID

"To dare is one option, facing FEAR in the eye and seeing who is stronger."

Dr. Bak Nguyen

0542

FROM LEVERAGE COMMUNICATION INTO SUCCESS

"Leadership is the capability to make people see the big picture and to make them believe in it."

Dr. Bak Nguyen

0543

FROM LEVERAGE COMMUNICATION INTO SUCCESS

"Make them feel the ride and the hope."

Dr. Bak Nguyen

0544

FROM LEVERAGE COMMUNICATION INTO SUCCESS

"To believe in the future is not to lie. But not at all!"

Dr. Bak Nguyen

0545

FROM LEVERAGE COMMUNICATION INTO SUCCESS

"They all believed in me because I believed first."

Dr. Bak Nguyen

0546

FROM LEVERAGE COMMUNICATION INTO SUCCESS

"Humble and confident!
Those are the qualities of a true leader."

Dr. Bak Nguyen

0547

FROM LEVERAGE COMMUNICATION INTO SUCCESS

"Sometimes do it, not because you wanted it but because of what you communicate..."

Dr. Bak Nguyen

0548

FROM LEVERAGE COMMUNICATION INTO SUCCESS

"Know what you need and what you want and act accordingly."

Dr. Bak Nguyen

0549

FROM FORCES OF NATURE

"If I don't know it yet, I'll find out later.
I did it because I felt it."

Dr. Bak Nguyen

0550

FROM FORCES OF NATURE

"Even if they don't like me,
that doesn't mean that I'll stop caring."

Dr. Bak Nguyen

0551

FROM THE BOOK OF LEGENDS, VOLUME 1

"To project is not the same than to pretend.
To project is to say what will be.
To pretend is to say what is not
and will never be."

Dr. Bak Nguyen

0552

FROM SELFMADE

"Leadership is a burden hard to share."

Dr. Bak Nguyen

0553

FROM SELFMADE

"The main trade that we should transmit
is the mean to adapt, the desire to reshape
and the ability to ask questions. "

Dr. Bak Nguyen

0554

FROM SELFMADE

"I do not rebuild, I build better, stronger, bigger!"

Dr. Bak Nguyen

0555

FROM SELFMADE

"You attract what you are and what you project."

Dr. Bak Nguyen

0556

FROM SELFMADE

"I refuse to average my intelligence and my passion just for the sake of loyalty and averaging."

Dr. Bak Nguyen

0557

FROM SELFMADE

"Every time you judge, you chip a little part of your soul."

Dr. Bak Nguyen

0558

FROM SELFMADE

"To give more than you take, that's the secret to leverage on your entourage and to build momentum."

Dr. Bak Nguyen

0559

FROM SELFMADE

"Nothing is more contagious than energy since we are always thirsty for it."

Dr. Bak Nguyen

0560

FROM THE RISE OF THE UNICORN

"Share to dream. dream to make a difference."

Dr. Bak Nguyen

0561

FROM THE RISE OF THE UNICORN

"March and people will be joining."

Dr. Bak Nguyen

0562

FROM THE RISE OF THE UNICORN

"It was about sharing a vision, not selling dreams."

Dr. Bak Nguyen

0563

FROM THE RISE OF THE UNICORN

"I won't stop until you, until we, until I, am happy."

Dr. Bak Nguyen

0564

FROM CHAMPION MINDSET

"Leadership is a matter of opinion, experience at best, not knowledge."

Dr. Bak Nguyen

0565

FROM CHAMPION MINDSET

"If you are doing the same thing over and over as an entrepreneur, that's your cue to hire more people and to start delegating."

Dr. Bak Nguyen

0566

FROM CHAMPION MINDSET

"Show the fullness to keep people inspired and lead the way to abundance."

Dr. Bak Nguyen

0567

FROM HOW TO WRITE A BOOK IN 30 DAYS

"Writing is about being confident."

Dr. Bak Nguyen

0568

FROM KRYPTO

" Can we do that? Only if we want to. I have something stronger, I can. "

Dr. Bak Nguyen

0569

FROM POWER, EMOTIONAL INTELLIGENCE

"Know you who are talking to, know yourself, and then, only then, deal."

Dr. Bak Nguyen

0570

FROM POWER, EMOTIONAL INTELLIGENCE

"It's not about you; it's about them."

Dr. Bak Nguyen

0571

FROM POWER, EMOTIONAL INTELLIGENCE

"The pain has to be greater than the pain of change for you to gain INFLUENCE with the least resistance. "

Dr. Bak Nguyen

0572

FROM POWER, EMOTIONAL INTELLIGENCE

"Help people, and you are on the right path of INFLUENCE. Don't argue, look into your heart."

Dr. Bak Nguyen

0573

FROM POWER, EMOTIONAL INTELLIGENCE

"What has changed, though, is that now, it is up to me to set the expectations!"

Dr. Bak Nguyen

0574

FROM POWER, EMOTIONAL INTELLIGENCE

"The easiest way to implement change is without resistance."

Dr. Bak Nguyen

0575

FROM POWER, EMOTIONAL INTELLIGENCE

"To be bold is part of the charm of the leadership!"

Dr. Bak Nguyen

0576

FROM POWER, EMOTIONAL INTELLIGENCE

"Justice is not to give to those who have not, but to give to those worthy."

Dr. Bak Nguyen

0577

FROM POWER, EMOTIONAL INTELLIGENCE

"Only be being kind and by believing that one can hope of a better future."

Dr. Bak Nguyen

0578

FROM BRANDING

"It's all a matter of wording, not the one you use but the one people feel."

Dr. Bak Nguyen

0579

FROM HORIZON VOLUME ONE

"Find usefulness to each situation, even the bad ones. You are there already."

Dr. Bak Nguyen

0580

FROM HOW TO NOT FAIL AS A DENTIST

"A team is a structure made of people. Structure and people, it takes the two to make a team."

Dr. Bak Nguyen

0581

FROM HOW TO NOT FAIL AS A DENTIST

"The main bond between you and your staff is a transactional one. The respect and the consideration also, but a transactional monetary one that is defining their place in society."

Dr. Bak Nguyen

0582

FROM MINDSET ARMORY

"It's not about being right, but about moving ahead."

Dr. Bak Nguyen

0583

FROM MINDSET ARMORY

"In a word, serve by empowering, not ordering."

Dr. Bak Nguyen

0584

FROM MINDSET ARMORY

"Dream big enough to empower the dreams of others."

Dr. Bak Nguyen

0585

FROM HUMILITY FOR SUCCESS

"Humility and Confidence are parents to Leadership."

Dr. Bak Nguyen

0586

FROM HUMILITY FOR SUCCESS

"The writings are on the walls, in the sky and all the books. But yet, we did otherwise, listening to people instead of reading."

Dr. Bak Nguyen

0587

FROM HUMILITY FOR SUCCESS

"Influence is to guide people through your actions, not only words."

Dr. Bak Nguyen

0588

FROM HUMILITY FOR SUCCESS

"To bow down to the average is not kindness,
it is intimidation and stupidity!"

Dr. Bak Nguyen

0589

FROM HUMILITY FOR SUCCESS

"People will bow and embrace what they feel,
nothing else."

Dr. Bak Nguyen

0590

FROM MASTERMIND

"If I don't have much values (burdens), it becomes
much easier not to impose those
on anyone else also."

Dr. Bak Nguyen

0591

FROM MASTERMIND

"Doubt is the biggest bluff in Life."

Dr. Bak Nguyen

0592

FROM THE ENERGY FORMULA

"To connect is paradoxical."

Dr. Bak Nguyen

0593

FROM PLAYBOOK INTRODUCTION VOLUME 1

"Leadership is to create actions and results from an ideas and words."

Dr. Bak Nguyen

0594

FROM PLAYBOOK INTRODUCTION VOLUME 1

"Leadership attracts, you will find love, success, sex, friendship and many more things on the way."

Dr. Bak Nguyen

0595

FROM PLAYBOOK INTRODUCTION VOLUME 2

"Networking is a two sides trade. You need to open up and deliver, but you also need to be humble enough to reach out."

Dr. Bak Nguyen

0596

FROM PLAYBOOK INTRODUCTION VOLUME 2

"To ignored, that's the ultimate insult."

Dr. Bak Nguyen

0597

FROM AMONGST THE ALPHAS, VOLUME 2

"There is nothing worse than regret to break a spirit."

Dr. Bak Nguyen

0598

FROM AMONGST THE ALPHAS, VOLUME 2

"The truth can be cold and hard, not everyone can survive it, that's why we created realities."

Dr. Bak Nguyen

0599

FROM AMONGST THE ALPHAS, VOLUME 2

"Networking gives us the means to bridge through space and time."

Dr. Bak Nguyen

0600

FROM AMONGST THE ALPHAS, VOLUME 2

"I will show you. I won't force you. But I won't wait for you."

William Bak and Dr. Bak Nguyen

0601

FROM AMONGST THE ALPHAS, VOLUME 2

"Give and grow. I never said sacrifice."

Dr. Bak Nguyen

0602

FROM SUCCESS IS A CHOICE

"To point out the problem may be the beginning,
but it will never build bridges."

Dr. Bak Nguyen

0603

FROM SUCCESS IS A CHOICE

"Everyone wants to be useful, to be served,
to feel important or to be listen to.
It is always one of the above."

Dr. Bak Nguyen

0604

FROM SUCCESS IS A CHOICE

"It is not true that a locomotive alone will go faster.
On paper yes, but after a short while, it will
lack the desire to keep pushing."

Dr. Bak Nguyen

0605

FROM RISING

"Nothing of worth is worth doing alone.
I keep going and welcome the company on the way."

Dr. Bak Nguyen

0606

FROM RISING

"The answer is a simple one, a noble one: make it about them, all about them!"

Dr. Bak Nguyen

0607

FROM AFTERMATH

"Leading is not about power, it s about courage."

Dr. Bak Nguyen

0608

FROM AFTERMATH

"Be that infrastructure, that bridge between profit and community."

Dr. Bak Nguyen

0609

FROM AFTERMATH

"Leadership is not to seize control but to inspire the control in others. Now, change control for empowerment."

Dr. Bak Nguyen

0610

FROM AFTERMATH

"Taking care of other people's problem, you have leverage and no liability. This is your way to score with least resistance."

Dr. Bak Nguyen

0611

FROM RELEVANCY

"Don't ask someone to be what one is not."

Dr. Bak Nguyen

0612

FROM RELEVANCY

"One cannot be a true leader with a small heart..."

Dr. Bak Nguyen

0613

FROM RELEVANCY

"We spent our entire life trying to beat the average, now, in a leadership position, our role is now to fight to raise the average."

Dr. Bak Nguyen

0614

FROM RELEVANCY

"The edges to win this war is our collectiveness and diversity, with humility, sharing and flexibility."

Dr. Bak Nguyen

0615

FROM MIDAS TOUCH

"Feel! That's the way to connect. Share, that's the way to keep the connection going."

Dr. Bak Nguyen

0616

FROM MIDAS TOUCH

" Friends and peers!"

Dr. Bak Nguyen

0617

FROM THE POWER OF DR

"I influenced people and people influenced me."

Dr. Bak Nguyen

0618

FROM TORNADO

"Anyone can burst and dare. But it will take much more to be a leader and a lasting change for good."

Dr. Bak Nguyen

0619

FROM EMPOWERMENT

"Do not expect people to be more than they are. You are doing yourself a favour."

Dr. Bak Nguyen

0620

FROM THE MODERN WOMAN

"Since women have bigger hearts, make sure to connect first before communicating."

Dr. Bak Nguyen

0621

FROM THE MODERN WOMAN

"A relation is about bonding, not negotiating."

Dr. Bak Nguyen

0622

FROM THE UAX STORY

"If you want to change the world, it has to be on an individual basis, otherwise it is just bullying."

Dr. Bak Nguyen

0623

FROM THE UAX STORY

"Nothing of worth is worth doing alone.
I welcome, but i won't wait."

Dr. Bak Nguyen

0624

FROM ALPHA LADDERS VOLUME ONE

"Big brother is not a status, but a role.
To keep its relevancy, one must always be ahead."

Dr. Bak Nguyen

0625

FROM ALPHA LADDERS VOLUME ONE

"Build from the differences, with FLEXIBILITY and COMPASSION. You are now holding in your hand the power of ABUNDANCE."

Dr. Bak Nguyen

0626

FROM ALPHA LADDERS VOLUME ONE

"Only by sharing, you are leaving imprints of your frequency."

Dr. Bak Nguyen

0627

FROM THE RISE OF THE UNICORN VOLUME TWO

"People buy how-to. Everyone does."

Dr. Bak Nguyen

0628

FROM THE RISE OF THE UNICORN VOLUME TWO

"Sharing my secrets to success, that's both the best opener, recruiter, and retainer."

Dr. Bak Nguyen

0629

FROM THE RISE OF THE UNICORN VOLUME TWO

"I drive and I learn."

Dr. Bak Nguyen

0630

FROM POWERPLAY

"Even if you are good, with a team, you can become great! If you are already great, with a team, you could last forever!"

Dr. Bak Nguyen

0631

FROM POWERPLAY

"Leadership has nothing to do with being bossy."

Dr. Bak Nguyen

0632

FROM POWERPLAY

"Give your team a challenge and a clear direction, and trust them to make you proud. Then, be there to empower and to help them on their mission."

Dr. Bak Nguyen

0633

FROM POWERPLAY

"If I have to be your boss, it is the beginning of the end of our relationship."

Dr. Bak Nguyen

0634

FROM POWERPLAY

"Do not tolerate or average down. Inspire, and empower."

Dr. Bak Nguyen

0635

FROM POWERPLAY

"In a leadership position, you are empowering, not ordering."

Dr. Bak Nguyen

0636

FROM POWERPLAY

"Make your team your best success.
Then, elevate them into your ambassadors."

Dr. Bak Nguyen

0637

FROM POWERPLAY

"Look for compatibility, for reassurance when hiring people, and always keep in mind the customers' point of view. They are the real bosses, at the end of the day."

Dr. Bak Nguyen

0638

FROM POWERPLAY

"A team is dynamic, engage them in your vision, empower them to make the difference, and keep them busy."

Dr. Bak Nguyen

0639

FROM POWERPLAY

"Inspire your team, empower them, and trust them to surprise you. That's how you will keep them engaged and motivated."

Dr. Bak Nguyen

0640

FROM POWERPLAY

"Equal and diverse."

Dr. Bak Nguyen

0641

FROM POWERPLAY

"That's the hardest part, to trust someone else with our weaknesses."

Dr. Bak Nguyen

0642

FROM POWERPLAY

"I am looking for harmony and synergy."

Dr. Bak Nguyen

0643

FROM POWERPLAY

"Balancing the forces has proven to be my best moves as a leader."

Dr. Bak Nguyen

0644

FROM POWERPLAY

"My team, mentors and partners are my greatest secrets to keep overachieving."

Dr. Bak Nguyen

0645

FROM 1SELF

"In a hurry, be the key
and let the system to others."

Dr. Bak Nguyen

0646

FROM ALPHA LADDERS VOLUME 2

"Leave vision to those who see without forcing.
Leave execution to those who will get it done
within a breeze."

Dr. Bak Nguyen

0647

FROM ALPHA LADDERS VOLUME 2

"Give intelligence to a man of heart and
you will find wisdom."

Dr. Bak Nguyen

0648

FROM MIRRORS

"To have a vision is to have the chance
to redefine yourself and the future."

Dr. Bak Nguyen

0648

FROM ALPHA LADDERS VOLUME 2

"We should resist the idea of immediate change to limit the resistance and the collaterals."

Dr. Bak Nguyen

0649

FROM THE BOOK OF LEGENDS VOLUME 3

"Take your work seriously, not yourself."

Dr. Bak Nguyen

0650

FROM MIRRORS

"I do not choose anymore, I embrace, and I prioritize."

Dr. Bak Nguyen

0651

FROM THE CONFESSION OF AN OVERACHIEVER

"No two people are exactly the same but very few will leave the tracks and the templates."

Dr. Bak Nguyen

0652

FROM THE CONFESSION OF AN OVERACHIEVER

"Know who you are first to be available to others."

Dr. Bak Nguyen

0653

FROM TO OVERACHIEVER EVERYTHING BEING LAZY

"Each and everyone has an agenda. It does not mean that we can join forces and work together."

Dr. Bak Nguyen

This is **Shortcut volume 3, LEADERSHIP**. Welcome to the Alphas.

PART 3

"SOCIETY"

by Dr. BAK NGUYEN

How to serve Society without being swallowed, that's the question. That's what I found to start this chapter in force in comparison to what is Society. The reason that I chose this angle is because of my mindset:

"If I can't do anything about it, I don't care."
Dr. Bak Nguyen

This quote goes back to my first book, **SYMPHONY OF SKILLS**. I still stand by it after a crazy ride writing close to 100 books, 2400 + quotes, and 2 Million words.

Society is what it is. We can influence it in the long run, but no one can change Society on his or her own within a short time frame. I am looking for quick wins and angles that I can tackle with speed and power.

Serving and empowering society were for me the best approaches to Society. Many, many times over, you read from me that Conformity and Society shaped and scarred me. Well, I may never make peace with Conformity, but Society is a different story.

Society is not a philosophy but a delicate balance to make a whole of the multiple and diverse individuals composing it while Conformity is the willpower to erase individuality, favouring the average. And that's what I have a hard time with, Conforming to the average.

Society may not be perfect but we must recognize that talking about Society, we had the wrong wording. Perfection is an opinion fixed in time while Society is the medley of all the opinions coming together. As far as we are talking of Society, it is harmony and balance that we should be talking about, not perfection.

And this is why I spent time and empowering not just the individuals but Society also. Even if I have at heart the development of the individual, hoping to see leaders emerge, I do believe that the only way to rise without or with fewer resistance is by empowerment and the betterment of the world.

That's the wording that I will use here, **WORLD** instead of **Society**. The reason is simple, Society might have somehow averaged or even limited our personal dream and rise. The term Society may have a bad reputation as opposed to the concept of **WORLD** which is used as our home and a symbol of **UNITY**.

"That's the keys, world, and unity."
Dr. Bak Nguyen

That's quote #2439. Our home, it might not be perfect but we love it, it is what we know and what made us into who we are. It is also the place in which we will be welcoming our children and pass down the legacy we received a few decades earlier.

This is my way to empower the world with love and gratitude. If I've been hurt and repressed by doctrines and philosophies, those can be challenged and changed for the betterment of the world.

So yes, I am giving my all to the world, to our world. This is also how I found my powers, empowering people and empowering the world. Doing so, I gained much influence with minimum resistance.

So the question was how to serve Society without being swallowed by it? Serve the individuals and their rise. On a societal level, don't ask for permission, and don't wait for people to ask for your help before jumping in. It is your home and the future of all, if you can make a difference, do it and react to your own ripple effect.

Keep in mind that every time that you are asking for permission, you are asking the present management for their approval to bring in change. You are addressing the wrong public!

In the previous chapter, I covered the difference between **POWER** and **INFLUENCE**. Well, if you are looking to make a difference, the management (**POWER**) will only listen to whatever changes that you are proposing if the pain was out of control and they are scared of the outcome.

"The pain has to be greater than the pain of change,
for change to occur."
Dr. Bak Nguyen

I don't know about you but to me, that is thinking backward. If I was looking to be a hero, I will wait for people to come in begging, and then, whatever solution I have will be welcomed. But this is the **WORLD** that we are talking about, my home and future, mine and those of my child! So no, I will not wait for the pain to be that great before proposing a change.

If my concern is to defend my home and future, the **WORLD**, thinking as such, I am in a direct collision course with Society (**POWER** and **MANAGEMENT**). This is a fight that I have no interest on taking on. I am no coward but I am no fool either, my energy and time are much needed elsewhere. This is what I meant by ***fewer resistance***.

"I don't look to be right but to win."
Dr. Bak Nguyen

Winning is almost impossible for a single person facing Society. I am not saying that it cannot be done but the odds are too slim and the commitment too long for a *sprinter* like me. I choose my fight. Writing these words, I hate the word **FIGHT**, I much prefer the words **BUILDING** and **HOPE**.

"Building hope to unify the world."
Dr. Bak Nguyen

That's the 2440th quote. Those are the words coming out of this chapter, **BUILDING**, **HOPE**, **UNITY**, and **WORLD**. If you are looking to serve Society without being swallowed, that is your recipe.

BUILDING, you need a vision, which is to see something that is not yet. Even if you might find support eventually, you will stand on your own for a while before finding support. People love to bet on the past, rarely on the future. It is again a question of wording, **RISK** versus **OPPORTUNITY**. So building, you must be ready to stand on your own for a while. Not a chance of being swallowed here.

HOPE, you need to feel that, day in and day out. You need to embody the belief that it is possible. If **VISION** was about what to do, **HOPE** is about to keep the spirit up against the people, the winds, and the odds, until your are proven right. And then, that's is part of the past. We, we are all about the future.

So yes, **HOPE** is carried by leaders, by drivers. Once more, you are safe from getting swallowed, unless to fall to intimidation or corruption.

UNITY, this is the only way to keep your vision up to last and to be of use. If what you are building serves people, people will empower it. The more people you empower, the stronger the **UNITY** that you are gathering, the lesser your chances of being swept away.

I don't ask people for permission, I asked them for their desires and needs (desires first, needs, second) and I listen carefully. Where I can help, I will. This is how I cut through the crap of resistance and denials. I am too lazy for the alternative. That said, I am serving my peers and, by extension, Society.

"Being lazy does not mean that you don't have to do shit.
It means that you don't have to go through shit
to get things done."
Dr. Bak Nguyen

Using that mindset, I also find a way to overcome most of the resistance. When I have to face one of my own pain, it is never easy, since I have to face my own denial. I also have to deal with my emotions. As I am taking care of others, this is no denial on my part and the emotions are nothing but positive since they were coming to me for help.

And when I said do not wait nor ask for permission, propose your help and expertise and have people coming to you. Being a leader, you have to be proactive. Being at the service of others, you must learn to listen first. That's the definition of **EMPOWERMENT**.

WORLD, this is an easy one. How many times we forsaw what will happen and we did not act? How many times we had the solution and kept quiet? We all did because we were waiting for permission and because we were scared to impose ourselves.

Well, do we have the same reaction concerning our family, our friends, our home? Absolutely not! We feel concerned and will not wait until it is too late to say: "I knew it." or even worse: "I told you so." Those won't help anyone.

Forget **SOCIETY** and replace it with **WORLD**. You will feel the shift in mentality and proactivity. My loyalty is to the world and to tomorrow. As much as possible, I try to play with the management (**POWER**), not looking for a useless fight. This is how I rose, both in impact and influence.

I just want to precise a point here. I have nothing against management. We need management to balance and to keep Society running day after day. That said, the role of management is to keep things smooth and the average stable.

If you are an agent of change, even for good, you won't find allies in the management team. Even if they will eventually accept your solution, they will be busy managing the implementation and the transition, that even then, you are bothering them. This is not about being the good or bad guy, it is simply about understanding the nature of the role of each.

"Building hope to unify the world."
Dr. Bak Nguyen

So yes, Society is our home, the World is our home and responsibility. If we all feel concerned and care, the world will be a better place! Doing so, we will all find our worth and legend!

This is **Shortcut volume 3, LEADERSHIP**. Welcome to the Alphas.

If I have changed the world from a dental chair,
you are all in a better position to change the world than I am.
Dr. BAK NGUYEN

PART 4

"89 SOCIETY QUOTES"

by Dr. BAK NGUYEN

1365

FROM SYMPHONY OF SKILLS

"They fear what they don't understand,
They hate what they can't have,
They will eat anything to ease their pain."

Dr. Bak Nguyen

1366

FROM IDENTITY, ANTHOLOGY OF QUESTS

"If people sing more, we will have less need of weapons and wars."

Dr. Bak Nguyen

1367

FROM IDENTITY, ANTHOLOGY OF QUESTS

"A citizen of the world bears his own weight. That's how he made a difference."

Dr. Bak Nguyen

1368

FROM IDENTITY, ANTHOLOGY OF QUESTS

"War is the affirmation of one's insecurity."

Dr. Bak Nguyen

1369

FROM CHANGING THE WORLD FROM A DENTAL CHAIR

"Loyalty is to a commitment, not to a person."

Dr. Bak Nguyen

1370

FROM MOMENTUM TRANSFER

" With much heat, even steel and be reshaped again into a new form. So is a doctrine."

Dr. Bak Nguyen

1371

FROM HYBRID

"With the definition of Freedom as we've been fed, Freedom is a liability."

Dr. Bak Nguyen

1372

FROM HYBRID

"Freedom is happiness, freedom is peace."

Dr. Bak Nguyen

1373

FROM HYBRID

"Rules are nothing but templates. Start with them and evolve from them."

Dr. Bak Nguyen

1374

FROM HYBRID

"To coexist, we discard the better part of the opposites, our ourselves."

Dr. Bak Nguyen

1375

FROM HYBRID

"...the loyal and the rebel..."

Dr. Bak Nguyen

1376

FROM REBOOT, TO GROW FROM MIDLIFE CRISIS

"Midlife Crisis is a product of our own creation, a side effect of our choices and our way of life."

Dr. Bak Nguyen

1377

FROM REBOOT, TO GROW FROM MIDLIFE CRISIS

"The family's unit is working, it's the couple that is suffering since both individuals are starving, feeding the family."

Dr. Bak Nguyen

1378

FROM LEVERAGE COMMUNICATION INTO SUCCESS

"You have gained a leverage in life, communicating to become a maestro conducting a harmony."

Dr. Bak Nguyen

1379

FROM LEVERAGE COMMUNICATION INTO SUCCESS

"Communication is a dance, of seduction, of control and of leverage."

Dr. Bak Nguyen

1380

FROM LEVERAGE COMMUNICATION INTO SUCCESS

"Communication is not just about leverage but also about programming."

Dr. Bak Nguyen

1381

FROM LEVERAGE COMMUNICATION INTO SUCCESS

"We all have the misconception that to communicate, one needs to talk."

Dr. Bak Nguyen

1382

FROM LEVERAGE COMMUNICATION INTO SUCCESS

"The easiest way to get your message through is to use the other party's words and thoughts."

Dr. Bak Nguyen

1383

FROM LEVERAGE COMMUNICATION INTO SUCCESS

"They were expressing, not communicating."

Dr. Bak Nguyen

1384

FROM LEVERAGE COMMUNICATION INTO SUCCESS

"Our body is built to push us looking for new encounters and connections. Our way to feed and grow."

Dr. Bak Nguyen

1385

FROM LEVERAGE COMMUNICATION INTO SUCCESS

"We replaced physical connections with a Number of digital likes and followers."

Dr. Bak Nguyen

1386

FROM LEVERAGE COMMUNICATION INTO SUCCESS

"Social Networks are means of empowerment and of addiction."

Dr. Bak Nguyen

1387

FROM LEVERAGE COMMUNICATION INTO SUCCESS

"Popularity has never been that affordable!"

Dr. Bak Nguyen

1388

FROM LEVERAGE COMMUNICATION INTO SUCCESS

"To break free from social pressure one must beat all expectations. "

Dr. Bak Nguyen

1389

FROM LEVERAGE COMMUNICATION INTO SUCCESS

"Free, but with a cost."

Dr. Bak Nguyen

1390

FROM FORCES OF NATURE

"As a society, we respect more authority than efficiency."

Dr. Bak Nguyen

1391

FROM FORCES OF NATURE

"To please them or to listen to ourselves,
that is the question?"

Dr. Bak Nguyen

1392

FROM THE BOOK OF LEGENDS, VOLUME 1

"Without giving, there is no taking.
That's the spirit of a team."

Dr. Bak Nguyen

1393

FROM SELFMADE

"Conformity is worst than karma, it is a bitch thinking
that only it holds the light."

Dr. Bak Nguyen

1394

FROM CHAMPION MINDSET

"When you are welcoming the world,
the world comes to you! All of the world!"

Dr. Bak Nguyen

1395

FROM CHAMPION MINDSET

"They will buy and vote for what they see and understand, not who you are."

Dr. Bak Nguyen

1396

FROM KRYPTO

"We may not be all equals, but as we received life, we should all have a chance to happiness and education. Our choices will make us equals or not."

Dr. Bak Nguyen

1397

FROM KRYPTO

"No system is perfect, in each and any of them, there are winners and, by extension, losers."

Dr. Bak Nguyen

1398

FROM KRYPTO

"Look, not for a perfect system but for the preservation and improvement upon what's there. To preserve, we must adapt and update."

Dr. Bak Nguyen

1399

FROM KRYPTO

" Perfection is nothing but a lie dearly paid in blood and sacrifices."

Dr. Bak Nguyen

1400

FROM KRYPTO

"Our world and happiness should be about sharing and love, not just comparing, judging and winning..."

Dr. Bak Nguyen

1401

FROM KRYPTO

"Helping others has made it way in my mind to draft solutions to save myself and those I love."

Dr. Bak Nguyen

1402

FROM KRYPTO

"Being a parent, there are many stories, many truths, and no safety net. There is no place for error."

Dr. Bak Nguyen

1403

FROM POWER, EMOTIONAL INTELLIGENCE

"In the game of society, make up your mind, are you playing defence or offence. There is not much in between."

Dr. Bak Nguyen

1404

FROM POWER, EMOTIONAL INTELLIGENCE

"To last, everything must be a two-way street."

Dr. Bak Nguyen

1405

FROM BRANDING

"The respect that I give to most is that I consider them as equals. My surprise is how often that I overestimated people… And my challenge is to keep doing so, with new people."

Dr. Bak Nguyen

1406

FROM HORIZON VOLUME TWO

"I came, I saw and I learnt, hopefully never to repeat the past."

Dr. Bak Nguyen

1407

FROM MINDSET ARMORY

"There is no more obvious insecurity than to try to make everyone alike."

Dr. Bak Nguyen

1408

FROM AMONGST THE ALPHAS, VOLUME 2

"We are a savage and cruel species."

Dr. Bak Nguyen

1409

FROM AMONGST THE ALPHAS, VOLUME 2

"We love eunuchs as pets since it is our way to feel superior."

Dr. Bak Nguyen

1410

FROM AMONGST THE ALPHAS, VOLUME 2

"Western medicine is mainly to cut and to replace."

Dr. Bak Nguyen

1411

FROM AMONGST THE ALPHAS, VOLUME 2

"Scarcity is the root of most of our flaws, even violence."

Dr. Bak Nguyen

1412

FROM MASTERMIND

"The final cure to Conformity
is to get rid of all expectations."

Dr. Bak Nguyen

1413

FROM RISING

"Laws are double edges swords."

Dr. Bak Nguyen

1414

FROM RISING

"To leave no one behind is a dream, a dangerous
one, with the law of the AVERAGE."

Dr. Bak Nguyen

1415

FROM RISING

"By rising, we force the AVERAGE to draft a new
distribution curve. By sharing, we raise
the core of the AVERAGE up."

Dr. Bak Nguyen

1416

FROM RISING

"To me, there are no rules for the rich and those for the poor. There are ignorance and beliefs."

Dr. Bak Nguyen

1417

FROM AFTERMATH

"Nowadays, it isn't about justice, but perception. That's a new and sad reality."

Dr. Bak Nguyen

1418

FROM RELEVANCY

"COVID-19 also killed complacency, moderation and conservatism. Now it is about overachieving and dialogue."

Dr. Bak Nguyen

1419

FROM RELEVANCY

"The age of competition is over, the age of collaboration is now. Or no one will be left to hear any other title."

Dr. Bak Nguyen

1420

FROM RELEVANCY

"It is time to move DIVERSITY from trend to value. And once again, I am not talking about gender, race or age."

Dr. Bak Nguyen

1421

FROM RELEVANCY

"In given time, FEAR will dictate all the answers."

Dr. Bak Nguyen

1422

FROM RELEVANCY

"Too many have sacrificed too much for us to now let FEAR take it all away. Remember the fights of our forefathers and foremothers."

Dr. Bak Nguyen

1423

FROM RELEVANCY

"For a new world dialogue, not a new world order!"

Dr. Bak Nguyen

1424

FROM RELEVANCY

"Life is dynamic and so are our economy and society.
Can we stop trying to define them in stone?"

Dr. Bak Nguyen

1425

FROM RELEVANCY

"The Tsunami will clean everything below sea level...
in plain words, the relevancy level."

Dr. Bak Nguyen

1426

FROM HORIZON VOLUME THREE

"A wedding is the best opportunity to strengthen
relationships, beyond the bride and groom."

Dr. Bak Nguyen

1427

FROM EMPOWERMENT

"To compare or to connect. Those are the alternatives.
Choose who you are comparing with and
be open to connect."

Dr. Bak Nguyen

1428

FROM THE MODERN WOMAN

"Our world isn't perfect and might never be, that's the beauty of life, to always have room for improvement, for improvisation and adaptation."

Dr. Bak Nguyen

1429

FROM THE UAX STORY

"Even on the world stage,
it is such a small world after all."

Dr. Bak Nguyen

1430

FROM THE UAX STORY

"Peace, Abundance and Harmony can only be obtained through the respect of diversity and of the differences."

Dr. Bak Nguyen

1431

FROM TOUCHSTONE, LEVERAGING TODAY'S PSYCHOLOGICAL SMOG

"COVID rebooted the world. As the systems are restarting, we now experienced all of its effects simultaneously, good and bad."

Dr. Bak Nguyen

1432

FROM TOUCHSTONE, LEVERAGING TODAY'S PSYCHOLOGICAL SMOG

"The more one belongs, the more challenged is his esteem."

Dr. Bak Nguyen

1433

FROM ALPHA LADDERS VOLUME ONE

"Passion is the dedication to an idea or to yourself. Compassion is the dedication to others. And this is not an idea, but a universal law."

Dr. Bak Nguyen

1434

FROM 1SELF

"The virus shut down all resistance. It also created a void for hope."

Dr. Bak Nguyen

1435

FROM ALPHA LADDERS VOLUME 2

"This time it is not about my like and dislike, but about empowerment and sustainability."

Dr. Bak Nguyen

1436

FROM ALPHA LADDERS VOLUME 2

"No system is ever perfect. No execution is ever perfect. All we can do is to keep polishing and adapting."

Dr. Bak Nguyen

1437

FROM ALPHA LADDERS VOLUME 2

"No matter the ideology,
the execution will leave its imprints."

Dr. Bak Nguyen

1438

FROM ALPHA LADDERS VOLUME 2

"Power corrupts, power enslaves,
despite all, power is charming."

Dr. Bak Nguyen

1439

FROM ALPHA LADDERS VOLUME 2

"That's maybe democracy, but that's also much waste of time, morale, and resources."

Dr. Bak Nguyen

1440

FROM ALPHA LADDERS VOLUME 2

"Can we celebrate the peaceful, uneventful lives too? Can we celebrate peace? Yes, we must."

Dr. Bak Nguyen

1441

FROM ALPHA LADDERS VOLUME 2

"ONE is the curse of our culture."

Dr. Bak Nguyen

1442

FROM ALPHA LADDERS VOLUME 2

"The culture of ONE and the corruption of power."

Dr. Bak Nguyen

1443

FROM THE BOOK OF LEGENDS VOLUME 3

"Entitlement is the flaw of liberty."

Dr. Bak Nguyen

1444

FROM THE BOOK OF LEGENDS VOLUME 3

"If everyone looks alike,
where are the fun and traction?"

Dr. Bak Nguyen

1445

FROM MIRRORS

"to face society is the first challenge one must face."

Dr. Bak Nguyen

1446

FROM THE CONFESSION OF AN OVERACHIEVER

"Conformity made sure that we are all aiming for the same things, in the same direction, with the same handicaps."

Dr. Bak Nguyen

1447

FROM TO OVERACHIEVER EVERYTHING BEING LAZY

"Trends are always true and trends happen with numbers, big numbers."

Dr. Bak Nguyen

1803

FROM SYMPHONY OF SKILLS

"Diversity is not who you are, but what you bring to the table."

Dr. Bak Nguyen

1804

FROM SYMPHONY OF SKILLS

"Entrepreneurs, you are crazy
not to embrace diversity."

Dr. Bak Nguyen

1805

FROM THE BOOK OF LEGENDS, VOLUME 1

"I live and let live, that's my mantra
Until now, I had a great Life."

Dr. Bak Nguyen

1806

FROM HORIZON VOLUME THREE

"Being secure allows tolerance and diversity.
Without fear, there is no hate and without hate,
we can build on the differences."

Dr. Bak Nguyen

1807

FROM THE MODERN WOMAN

"What she though was communication, I perceived as
micro-managing. What she took as collaborating,
I perceived as perpetual negotiations."

Dr. Bak Nguyen

1808

FROM POWERPLAY

"Empower diversity into ambassador and balance the systems, this is the secret of building a perfect team."

Dr. Bak Nguyen

This is **Shortcut volume 3, LEADERSHIP**. Welcome to the Alphas.

If I have changed the world from a dental chair,
you are all in a better position to change the world than I am.

Dr. BAK NGUYEN

PART 5

"ALPHA"

by Dr. BAK NGUYEN

Alphas, what an interesting subject. Is the question of this chapter should be what is an Alpha or how does one become an Alpha? Well, even if those are 2 different questions, they lead to the same exact answer!

Alpha means first in order. The first, not the best. By the law of consequences the first, if they survive the initial assault, often grow to become the best. What made it possible was to start (first) but the key to the equation was to **GROW**.

"No one is born the best, but everyone can be the first to start."
Dr. Bak Nguyen

If that is so, why are **ALPHAS** so hated before they are idolized? We covered that in the **SOCIETY** chapter, peers do not like one of them breaking the ranks of the average, and the average moves in herds, as an average.

"SOCIETY and those in control (management) hate to play catch up with those ahead, even if they are the ones raising the average and, by extension, Society itself."
Dr. Bak Nguyen

That's quote #2441. Haven't I told you not to wait for permission to make a difference? Well, that's the nature of an Alpha, to make a difference or to refuse to stay idle in facing a problem, an injustice or an inefficiency.

We all have in us the potential and desire to act. Sooner or later, we will follow up on these instincts of ours to move forward. That's our Alphaness inside boiling. In other words, we all have the potential to be Alphas.

That said, we are not always **ALPHAS**, even if we took the lead at some point. **ALPHANESS** is not a status or a nature, but a state of mind as the body and the heart overcome the mind and its conditioned from Conformity and/or fear.

We act because our body and hormones propel us forward. After the events are solved or have passed, our hormones and body will cease pushing and most of us will resume back to who we were.

Not exactly. Think of the hormones as a Tsunami striking from inside. Until that point, we build our internal **DAM** higher and higher to contain our emotions and hormones.

Except for the **DAM**, nothing else was getting bigger. As you are releasing the Tsunami, now the rest of your systems will have to adapt to the influx of energy. That is what propelling you forward.

Well, after the event, these systems have grown and will not shrink down anytime soon. They are ready for more. And that's the pivot moment where one will decide to keep feeding his or her systems (growth) or to resume to feed the internal **DAM**.

"ALPHANESS is not a status but a state of mind…
until it becomes a choice."
Dr. Bak Nguyen

Think of your body as a city. What happens when your city is chosen to hold the next Olympic games? Well, your city received attention and funds to prepare to host the international event. It might take billion of dollars and years of preparation but you will upgrade your city to the state of the art and trends, only to be ready to host.

The Olympics will be hosted successfully. People from all around the world will come, see, experience, and talk about their unique experience in your city. You have their attention and have gained much influence (**ALPHA**).

Then, at the end of the games, they will leave and the Olympic committee will choose the next city for the next games. You will pass on the flame (**ALPHANESS**) to the next city.

But your newly upgraded infrastructures, they are not going anywhere. Now they can be great assets to leverage to keep propelling your evolution or they can become burdens and liabilities on your treasury. Yes, everything needs maintenance.

If in the case of a person, we are talking about that state as a choice, in the case of a city, it is a question of vision, of leadership. Since the upgrades have been financed with tax dollars and often rolled into a long-term debt, it does not make any sense to cease utilizing them, even less, to let them to decay.

The picture is clear, but to the human body and mind, it is not about tax dollars, but the influx of hormones that will or will not keep the **ALPHA** state up and running.

So now you understand the phenomena of the awakening and of someone's moment (the day his or her Tsunami will break the **DAM**). That will happen to everyone sooner or later. The difference is what are we doing with the infrastructures after the Olympics.

And what is the difference between the **ALPHA** stage and **GROWTH**? Well, growing, we are doing that inside of the wall of our **DAM**. Acting as an Alpha, we are now growing outside of the **DAM**. In other words, you can train and evolve as much as you want, but until you are coming out and put that to good use, no one will care. Even you will give up on your training eventually!

HEALING was to acknowledge our desires and emotions (Tsunami). **GROWING** was to train and get prepare (within the containment of the **DAM**). Now, to be a leader, an agent of change (**ALPHA**), one must break the **DAM** and go out (in **SOCIETY**) to put his power (**GROWTH**) to solve a problem of the collective. Then, his growth will be both internal (power and skills) and external (**INFLUENCE**). That's the Alpha state.

After that episode, the choice to keep feeding the growth externally (influence and the betterment of the world) will make that person into a leader. The alternative is to resume back to repair and to upgrade the **DAM** and to make sure that it will contain the next Tsunami. Even worse, some will go as far as to go to the source of the Tsunami and sabotage its formation.

Keep in mind that the power of the Tsunami is from the same source that is keeping your heart beating each day, day after day. To each our choices, to each our Destiny.

This should clarify the question of what is an **ALPHA** and how do we become one. Alphaness is a natural state that will come, sooner or later. How to react to that is the main question. More importantly, what are we doing after the first Tsunami, will draft our Destiny into either a footnote or a legend.

It was not about us,
But about what we can do.
It was not about serving our needs
But those of others.

Alphaness is a state
Growth is a choice
Influence is a consequence.
We call that leadership.

Coming next are 42 states of **ALPHANESS** to guide you once your **DAM** breaks for the first time. And before I let you go, let me remind you that a Tsunami is energy released. It is might be powerful but it is neither good nor bad.

Yield it or not, that's your choice. Usually, what is good or bad, are the consequences and collateral of the passage of that force of nature. Yes, you hold in you a **force of nature**.

Yield it well and your legend will never fade. Let it run you and you will spent your days in remorses.

This is **Shortcut volume 3, LEADERSHIP**. Welcome to the Alphas.

If I have changed the world from a dental chair
you are in a better position to change the world than I am

Dr. BAK NGUYEN

PART 6

"42 ALPHA QUOTES"

by Dr. BAK NGUYEN

0354

FROM THE POWER BEHIND THE ALPHA

" She built the Alpha from the ground up, with her love."

Dr. Bak Nguyen

0355

FROM THE POWER BEHIND THE ALPHA

" Alpha is a state of mind of offering and volunteering, not servitude. Love and confidence will allow you to make the difference."

Dr. Bak Nguyen

0356

FROM THE POWER BEHIND THE ALPHA

" Being an Alpha is a choice, to find that nature from our childhood."

Dr. Bak Nguyen

0357

FROM THE POWER BEHIND THE ALPHA

"An Alpha is someone who made up his mind to be what nature intended for him to be."

Dr. Bak Nguyen

0358

FROM THE POWER BEHIND THE ALPHA

"To grow into an Alpha, you'll need love
to free yourself first and to heal."

Dr. Bak Nguyen

0359

FROM THE POWER BEHIND THE ALPHA

" The Alpha's attraction is the establishment
of a gravity centre."

Dr. Bak Nguyen

0360

FROM AMONGST THE ALPHAS, VOLUME 1

"Alphaness is not as status,
it is a choice and a state of mind."

Dr. Bak Nguyen

0361

FROM AMONGST THE ALPHAS, VOLUME 1

"No matter the intentions, Alphas will be aiming
for results. Judge them on the results,
not the intentions."

Dr. Bak Nguyen

0362

FROM AMONGST THE ALPHAS, VOLUME 1

"To Alphas, being and doing are important, while winning is a side effect. "

Dr. Bak Nguyen

0363

FROM AMONGST THE ALPHAS, VOLUME 1

"An Alpha is no gambler, even if the Alpha is a pretty darn good player."

Dr. Bak Nguyen

0364

FROM AMONGST THE ALPHAS, VOLUME 1

"Not all heroes are Alphas."

Dr. Bak Nguyen

0365

FROM AMONGST THE ALPHAS, VOLUME 1

"Unlike the rest of the world, you can't define an Alpha through his fear."

Dr. Bak Nguyen

0366

FROM AMONGST THE ALPHAS, VOLUME 1

"Alphas do not believe in perfection, they believe in results."

Dr. Bak Nguyen

0367

FROM AMONGST THE ALPHAS, VOLUME 1

"For Alphas, bigger is not necessarily better. To get things done swiftly is."

Dr. Bak Nguyen

0368

FROM AMONGST THE ALPHAS, VOLUME 1

"Alpha is a state of mind and a choice."

Dr. Bak Nguyen

0369

FROM AMONGST THE ALPHAS, VOLUME 1

"An Alpha is a state of mind, not a tactic nor a strategy."

Dr. Bak Nguyen

0370

FROM AMONGST THE ALPHAS, VOLUME 1

"Catch the ALPHA's enthusiasm and vibe and, as you are ready, start your own journey."

Dr. Bak Nguyen

0371

FROM AMONGST THE ALPHAS, VOLUME 1

"Alpha is another game with other rules, players, and gravity."

Dr. Bak Nguyen

0372

FROM AMONGST THE ALPHAS, VOLUME 1

"Alpha or not, the key to growth is to stay as open as possible. Take in, digest, and give back. Then repeat."

Dr. Bak Nguyen

0373

FROM AMONGST THE ALPHAS, VOLUME 1

"Everything changes and evolves, so will the Alphas, to keep their relevancy."

Dr. Bak Nguyen

0374

FROM AMONGST THE ALPHAS, VOLUME 1

"Alphas will always win the war, if not today, well, they will in a few generations."

Dr. Bak Nguyen

0375

FROM AMONGST THE ALPHAS, VOLUME 1

"For an Alpha, the answer is often from within..."

Dr. Bak Nguyen

0376

FROM AMONGST THE ALPHAS, VOLUME 1

"Being an Alpha is a state of mind. It has to be leveraged and put into motion to last."

Dr. Bak Nguyen

0377

FROM AMONGST THE ALPHAS, VOLUME 1

"Being an Alpha is being a champion."

Dr. Bak Nguyen

0378

FROM AMONGST THE ALPHAS, VOLUME 1

"To mentor an Alpha, one has to be an Alpha himself."

Dr. Bak Nguyen

0379

FROM AMONGST THE ALPHAS, VOLUME 1

"The worse that could happen to an Alpha is not to be alone, but to be surrounded by Betas with love."

Dr. Bak Nguyen

0380

FROM AMONGST THE ALPHAS, VOLUME 1

"To be an Alpha is a choice and a way of life. Life is Alpha, we were all born with the Alpha Gene."

Dr. Bak Nguyen

0381

FROM AMONGST THE ALPHAS, VOLUME 1

"Alphas are solution seekers, not trouble makers."

Dr. Bak Nguyen

0382

FROM AMONGST THE ALPHAS, VOLUME 1

"Alpha is not a status nor a title but a choice. The rest is the line of consequences following one's choice."

Dr. Bak Nguyen

0383

FROM AMONGST THE ALPHAS, VOLUME 1

"Stillness and stiffness will create authority. This has nothing to do with Alphaness."

Dr. Bak Nguyen

0384

FROM AMONGST THE ALPHAS, VOLUME 2

"Alpha, dragon, infinite, that was my way to greet you with fortune and hope."

Dr. Bak Nguyen

0385

FROM AMONGST THE ALPHAS, VOLUME 2

"The journey of the ALPHA is a lonely one."

Dr. Bak Nguyen

0386

FROM AMONGST THE ALPHAS, VOLUME 2

"The day I stop seeing my bellybutton, that day, I became an Alpha."

Dr. Bak Nguyen

0387

FROM AMONGST THE ALPHAS, VOLUME 2

"Being an Alpha is not to be the first, but to keep being. By being, I meant learning and doing."

Dr. Bak Nguyen

0388

FROM AMONGST THE ALPHAS, VOLUME 2

"The hope of an Alpha is within the beliefs that healing is possible."

Dr. Bak Nguyen

0389

FROM AMONGST THE ALPHAS, VOLUME 2

"I found my Alpha powers through love, without sacrifices."

Dr. Bak Nguyen

0390

FROM RELEVANCY

"The Alphas aren't just overachievers,
they are here because they are overachieving
and will keep doing so."

Dr. Bak Nguyen

0391

FROM ALPHA LADDERS VOLUME ONE

"Being an Alpha isn't about what I want.
It is not about being what I am either.
It comes down to what I can do."

Dr. Bak Nguyen

0392

FROM ALPHA LADDERS VOLUME ONE

This is not what I want. This is not who I am.
But this is what I can do, for you. So be it. Let's do it."

Dr. Bak Nguyen

0393

FROM ALPHA LADDERS VOLUME 2

"The role of the Alphas as an organization
is to nurture and to support the entrepreneur and
the leader as he or she is morphing
from vision into execution."

Dr. Bak Nguyen

0394

FROM ALPHA LADDERS VOLUME 2

"As Alphas, we show and compare our scars first, and then, we tell the story of these scars, good and bad."

Dr. Bak Nguyen

0395

FROM ALPHA LADDERS VOLUME 2

"From I to WE."

Dr. Bak Nguyen

This is **Shortcut volume 3, LEADERSHIP**. Welcome to the Alphas.

PART 7

"THE POWER OF QUOTES"

by Dr. BAK NGUYEN

The power of a quote is to deliver you with inspiration as you need it and in the form you are ready to welcome. As I said many times before, a quote is not a rhetoric exercise, it is an affirmation of a reality of life that might ease your way.

Going through my collection of thoughts allowed me to revisit my writing in a different light. Compiling them in the **SHORTCUT series**, it brought new life and a whole new perspective to my work.

From looking for a quick cheat, I fooled myself into the biggest undertaking task of my writing career so far, the sorting and filtering of my entire library. Actually, this is an understatement. What I was doing without being fully aware was to update the books to today's trends.

I cut my books into a smaller and smaller formats. Its content can now be scattered around and help, even the people who do not have the time to read an entire book. I don't judge you, I am one of you.

I started writing Ted Talks as chapters because never, I thought that I would be writing a book. So a chapter at a time, I built up the narrative, the audience, the momentum. Massing up to close to 100 books, it is time now to take the process in reverse.

"Let's deconstruct to reconstruct differently, even better."
Brenda Garcia

Writing the third volume of **SHORTCUT, LEADERSHIP (RISING)** after the first two volumes **HEALING** and **GROWTH**, is a privilege, the privilege to accompany you on your rise, your legend. As life happens a day at a time, we should be able to evolve a quote at a time.

We stood for so long with the idea that to learn and to evolve, one should leave to learn and train until ones is ready.

"Well, what I learnt from life is that we are never ready until we've done it."
Dr. Bak Nguyen

That's quote #2442. And to stop and take the time... well, if there is something of worth in this life is Time! The more we've spent it around, the better our understanding of that worth. So no, taking the time to learn something that may or may not be of use is not an option anymore. That's why we are at the crossroad as a Society, as a collective of individuals.

Technology and freedom show us the possibilities and the horizons. There are so many to choose from. In short, it is all possible, your wildest dreams and the dreams that you haven't even dreamt yet! That said, we are not there yet, we have just been shown a glimpse of what could be. And then, we see another one and another one. And this is where it becomes confusing.

Instead of empowering us to our best, we are now torn between the possibilities of a better future. Even worse, some of these futures are not even ours, they have been presented as a choice that we mistakenly took as a dream of ours. This is why, if time is scarce, it is necessary to take the time to slow down and to heal. That's **HEALING**.

Once healed, we can sort out who we are and what we are not. In other words, we now know our dreams from the multitude of glimpses offered. Now is time to **GROW**. Yes, growth will take time and that will happen inside of the confinement of our personal **DAM**, while we keep up the appearances and keep our place and function in Society.

A day at a time, a quote of a time, we are building up our Confidence. But then, the danger of being stuck in that mode for too long will have to be dealt with too! We were stuck for so long, the point was not to free ourselves to tie ourselves down again, only with different ropes.

That's when I discovered the hack to that built-in menace understanding the link between **GROWTH** and **SHARING**. And what do we share, opinions? Well, do that and you will be back to healing pretty soon. The only thing worth sharing is what can help the others, not an opinion but an experience of life, a story, a quote. In a word, **EMPOWERMENT**.

From one quote to the next, I found my powers empowering you. Keep growing, keep seeking for your worth and usefulness, and empower others, self-empowerment does not work.

"You can't grow much from the feelings and
the emotions coming from self-empowerment."
Dr. Bak Nguyen

That's quote #2443. So here I am, continuing my journey, empowering you a quote at a time, a quote inspiring you, easing your next move while not asking for the sacrifice of your time in return. This is the **POWER OF QUOTES**.

Here are 8 of my 77 famous quotes, the core of my growth and power. I will explain and share with you shortly their story, 8 at a time, respecting the number of the Dragon. May they inspire you and find their use in the palm of your hands.

FAMOUS QUOTE 1

0008

FROM INDUSTRIES' DISRUPTORS

"The day you are fighting to raise the average instead of beating it, that day, you've joined the leadership."

Dr. Bak Nguyen

I come from a family of immigrants. My family lost everything after, not one, but two wars. I am the 3rd generation having to build from the ground up. Regrets, my parents and grandparents had them. We, we were born in a world of commitments, where the only option was to go up, we were already at the bottom.

So growing up, it was always a matter of being better to survive. Not simply being better, but being better than the person standing next to us. If we had no regrets, we were burden with another virus, **comparison**. To move up the ladder of society, working hard and being better than the guys next door.

And so we did, moving up the ladder one after the next. I was very fortunate to grow up in Canada, a country of freedom and opportunity, a country built on systems and the belief that everyone has the same chance to succeed.

Moving up the ladders meant to do good in school and to keep studying until you have a title, a function, a job. As a doctor in dental medicine, I took my place in society. That came with an exclusive licence to practice dental medicine and a line of credit. With these 2, I built and never looked back.

That's not completely true. I was efficient enough to have free time in between the busy curriculum of life as an immigrant dental student, to dream of making movies and of changing the world. I also had the chance to participate in a few of the events that could have changed the history of my country. History did not change, but I was as I contributed.

Long story short, I had a taste of power before I was 18. Then, I decided that it was not for me. That said, that changed me at my core. Suddenly, surviving was not the only option on the table anymore. Doing better than the guy next door will only lead that far.

I was a student without qualifications, an immigrant looking to fit in, and yet, I rose quickly in the eye of power and influence, because I cared. It will take me 10 years later before I could articulate what I learnt then into a quote, but it will become one of my signature quote: to raise the average instead of beating it!

Tell that to an immigrant, you will be ridiculed. Tell that to fellow students looking to be admitted in dental or med school, they will step all over you, maybe not in your face, but as soon as you have your back turn. Unfortunately, that's how Society set us up.

Has that changed once one gets into med or dental school? Not at all. To keep forging the best, competition and average (to beat) are the norm. And once graduated? Well, it is possible to change course, but it will be a long and painful journey to undo what has built us up to that point: excellence and being better than the average.

10 years down that road and I was pretty good beating the average. And then, ***Power*** called again. I was reminded of who I was and what I could do. Once again, I did not take the opportunity, but I was open to listen.

I was reminded that power and influence do not come from being the best, but from serving the many. I had a good taste of that as I built up a good life standard, servicing my patients, one at a time. Was it time to help people differently, with more efficiency?

Fast forward 10 more years, I turned down the possibility to run for office yet one more. But I am growing stronger and stronger, more and more influential. I did that because I cared. I care to raise the average. And I gained even more speed and momentum the day that I cease wasting time looking to beat the average.

FAMOUS QUOTE 2

0011

FROM INDUSTRIES' DISRUPTORS

"I believe in myself and I do it for God, not the other way around."

Dr. Bak Nguyen

I will be banned from entering churches and cult places once this quote is echoing. The first time that I said it out loud, I was still in dental school and going to church. To get closer and more familiar with his followers, the priests started to share their sermons with the audience.

When asked about how God is making an impact in my life, I stood up, took the microphone, and shared that I do not pray to ask for anything. I simply pray to either apologize or to say thank you. The audience was moved and rallied quickly with my words. It felt good, good to share, and good to be of help.

The non-verbal of the priest was hard to miss. Never again he will approach me. I just stole his thunder somehow... That's how it started, my awakening and my rise. After that one, I expand my horizons and look for my answers in all of Life and the Universe.

I healed, I grew and I found powers and momentum. I always told you that it was through **empowerment**. Well, from my childhood bathed in religion, I must say that there is one story that I kept close to my heart: from the bible, there is a story of a master and 3 servants. The master went away for a year and left to each of his servants, talents (money in roman's time).

3 talents to the first servant, 2 to the second, and 1 to the last. A year later, the master returned and asked for his servants. You know the story. Well, I had a nightmare once, showing up in front of God and waiting for my turn to show my return on the talents that I received. Very proudly and confident, I advanced and present to him the 3 talents received and 3 more created.

And then, God stood up. Angry, looking down on me he says: "What are you talking about, I gave you 10!" I woke up all wet. From that day on, that was the only fear I kept close to my heart. I ran faster and faster to not run of time and to deliver on those talents received.

Until it is over, I still have time to deliver more. And by the end, I will have no regret, if I am short, I will take the blame but won't have to apologize for it. And that is how God influences my life.

FAMOUS QUOTE 3

0026

FROM LEVERAGE COMMUNICATION INTO SUCCESS

"Find your worth in the service of others."

Dr. Bak Nguyen

In the same line of thoughts, how does one serves God? Well, I did that helping others. The story did not end with my realization that time is important. Both as a child of God and a doctor, my role is to heal those in need at the best of my abilities. I have to heal and I have to improve my abilities. I did both.

Not just attending dental seminars and perfecting my art as a surgeon but I did that also letting go of my pride and learning to listen to my patient and to understand their pain. Quickly, I realized that treating teeth and illnesses was the easy part.

Gaining their trust and building up their confidence were the main issues. You can heal a tooth, that's mechanical but it will break again if you did not have your patient part of the solution.

And I did, I opened myself up and learn to listen and to empower. Doing so, from an average dentist stuck with his choice, I became a loved and successful dentist, one looked up to by patients and colleagues.

Against all odds, I succeeded in a world and science that I despited. I have no love for treating teeth but I love my patients. This is how I can up with another signature quote: "I treat people, not teeth."

That slowly propelled me to have the trust of the financial world. Today, **Mdex & Co.**, my company, has a chance to change the dental industry and how dentistry will be delivered in the future. It is a long journey, but the seeds are growing wings, not roots, wings.

And the wings, they are coming from the **ALPHAS** that I met during the COVID war. And how do you think that I attracted so many people, so more powerful and smarter than I am? I did so, empowering them and looking for ways to raise the average.

Serve the others and you will find allies. And why allies are so important? Because they will help you lower the resistance to your presence and your achievements. While **HEALING**, you have to start that alone, **GROWING** can be made faster and easier with mentors and coaches, **RISING**, you will need allies to last and to prevail. Find your worth in the service of others and you will rise!

Well, let me make you laugh. We started this by saying that I was looking to honour God and making good on the talents that I've received. Well, here is a blessing/curse.

Every time that I pushed the limits and delivered, I discovered, at the end of the line, more powers! For a moment, I am ecstatic... and then, I realized that I will have to deliver on those too!

That kept me going ever since, happy and never contained, humble and grateful but always in a hurry to run against Time. Well, Time has become my greatest rival and companion.

FAMOUS QUOTE 4

0039

FROM HOW TO WRITE A BOOK IN 30 DAYS

"The fewer the words, the better."

Dr. Bak Nguyen

I might not be the right person to tell you this after close to 2 million words written but if you are still reading, you know that it is true. Actually, within my first few books, I was reproached that I spent just a phrase, maximum two, on an idea and I moved on to the next too quickly. I listened and adapted. If today, you see me repeating myself using different words, it is in response to that comment.

That is if I am varying my wordings around the same idea. If I am repeating the same exact words, the intent is much different. That is to mark your imagination and to pace your awakening, growth, or rise. But if there is something that I hate, it is to repeat myself or to walk the same path twice.

I don't believe in perfection, to do and to redo something until it is perfect. I believe in doing the best you can within the time and with resources in hand, to deliver, to learn, and to evolve. And the only way to evolve is to move on.

Coming back at the same thing to doing it better and better, you are looping yourself… I still have other talents on which I have to deliver, so no thank you, not for me.

Fewer the words, the better. This is absolutely true as you are telling a story or trying to appeal to people. Choose your wording carefully and have them to ask for more.

Then, you have their attention and you can now deploy more of your story and wording. Even then, I have too much respect for your time and mine, to go on and go.

To keep your interest and to honour your attention, I will always keep it as short as possible. This is how and why you are keep coming back, asking for more!

FAMOUS QUOTE 5

0043
FROM BRANDING
"Arrogance is not the bragging of our knowledge,
but rather the denial of our ignorance."
Dr. Bak Nguyen

I love this one! I was born different, confident. And then, family education, religion, and Conformity took over to forge me. All of my life, because I ask for questions above the pay grade of those in power, I've been brought down and marked as arrogant, even ridiculed as stupid and dump.

What they were looking for was obedience, blind obedience. I was blind and I was ready to learn and to collaborate, not just to obey. That said, I realize soon enough that going up against ***Management*** was not a battle that I could win. Not even a battle worth fighting.

So I kept my head low and conformed. I did what was asked of me. I pushed myself to outperform and to overdeliver on those to free myself for the scrutinize and enjoyed the free time to learn and evolve on my own.

They did not break me but within 20 years in that regime, I was somehow confused. Then, as I moved on and got mentors instead of professors to guide me, something stroke me at my core. All of my mentors agreed on the fact that they are surprised with how humble I was. Humble?! That's new, while all of my life, I got use to the labels of arrogant and dump.

Dump, I knew that it was just an insult but arrogant, that one stuck with me! That will take me years to finally understand the wisdom of my mentors. I was humble because I was always willing to learn and to seek new answers, even to the same questions. I was smart because I was flexible and keep growing at the minute.

And then, I meant with some of the most powerful minds that I had the privilege to meet. What others called arrogance, they call leadership! But before I could reach leadership, I needed to heal first.

To get rid of the denials, the false labels, and to accept. And that's your only way to your power, it is to accept who you are and what you are not… yet (if you choose so).

So I listened and healed. I accept who I was, acknowledged my past, my choices, and my talents. Those are what I am betting on. My weaknesses, I know them too, all too well. As much as possible, I do not bet on them but since they are part of me, I do my best not to step on them.

Is erasing weakness the best strategy? Maybe, but that will cost much in time. I prefer to compensate these weaknesses with ***overpowers*** that I found, elevating others. Then as the successes and experiences accumulated, either that weakness is now a tiny dot of the past or the excuse for my next quest.

All of that was made possible the day that I found my voice, my confidence. And that came the day that I understood that ***Humility and Confidence can co-exist***, even served in synergy! Arrogance, that's not a word in my lexicon anymore.

Accept who you are, nurture who you are, only you will, only you know, and once you have passed that state of you, only then, there can be an us.

FAMOUS QUOTE 6

0054

FROM PLAYBOOK INTRODUCTION VOLUME 1

"Nothing will last forever, and nothing is free."

Dr. Bak Nguyen

Do I really have to explain this one? And yet, you have no idea of how many people are still struggling with that one. Yes, there is a price to everything. What people don't know or take much time to understand is the nature of the currency and of each trade.

Time is our most precious resource. That's the only thing that we each have 24 hours of. Not everyone will have the same number of years but since that is not a knowledge that we possess in advance, we are all blessed with the bliss of ignorance on that one.

Talking of action and leadership, the ones moving forward are the ones who understand the value and worth of time and timing. Those left behind are often those looping in indecision or in the quest for perfection. There is no other way to see this one.

So why is it that some of us rise while others are staying behind? It is not about injustices or opportunities but our mindset facing a crossroad. At each crossroad, we have to make a decision. Even not making a decision is a decision. Beware of those you made by default.

The timing is always **NOW** since you are standing at that crossroad. Will you go left, right or even go back, that is your choice. You won't know for sure what is ahead until you have travelled the way.

You may take advice and opinions, which will take time off of your reserve. If you are doing that to save yourself the mistakes ahead, that's great. Sooner or later, you will arrive at a crossroad that nobody has travelled successfully before. So now what?

I am very grateful for the teaching, coaching, and mentoring that I have received and on which I leverage from, every day. That said, what I found useful to learn was not what they did but how they faced their challenges and how they stayed on top of their emotions. That's my mindset.

"If early on, I learnt art, craft, and science,
today, I listen to learn experiences and wisdom.
Those are what preparing me to face the unknown."
Dr. Bak Nguyen

That's quote #2444. So I learnt to not judge anyone to stay open and flexible. I also have to learn to sort out the facts from the opinions and the opinions from wisdom. That's how I spent my time and resource, on what I can leverage to move ahead.

And indecision and doubt, do I even have to cover those?

FAMOUS QUOTE 7

0065
FROM AFTERMATH
"In times of crisis, it is the perfect opportunity
to reinvent who we are."
Dr. Bak Nguyen

How do we move forward, no matter what? In the entertainment world, they have a great saying that the show must go on. Just like the earth will keep rotating and the sun will keep rising, we are part of a much bigger ensemble.

That said, rising, you are disrupting the present order of things. Until the pain is greater than the change that you are proposing, you are the pain! That's how most of the people and how ***Management*** will see you. You still have to walk your path.

But when a crisis hits, the Order is not anymore. From these cracks, new heroes, new figures, and new trends will emerge. Were you ready to ride the change? Whatever you answer, the change is still happening and you are part of it.

If you are already in your awakening, that crisis is simply new and fresh data to compile as you are growing. You won't even have to break the wall of your **DAM**, the crisis did that for you. Now the only question is, will you ride the change or be ran by it. The sooner you understand this one, the easier, or at least, less harder, will be your next journey.

And of course, within a crisis that is big enough to unbalance the present order, no one is ready. You are at the crossroad where no one has even come back from. What do you do? Time is your resource.

I won't tell you what to do, just share with you what I did. I stayed open and flexible and I moved forward. I was doing that before the COVID war, adapting and moving fast in unknown territories.

When COVID hit, I was smashed as everybody else. But adapting I knew and denial, I knew all but too well to embrace, so I reinvented myself with what was left available and I leveraged my way through. I became the host of the **ALPHAS**. History will tell what will be next.

FAMOUS QUOTE 8

0075

FROM TO OVERACHIEVER EVERYTHING BEING LAZY

"Nowadays, influence is power without liability."

Dr. Bak Nguyen

Rising, what you should be aware of is the resistance. This is what might break you. Remember the law of physic stating that to every force, there is one opposite force of equal value?

Well, put differently, because you are rising, you are also causing the rise of your demise or at least, rival. Unless that force was not one that can be identified, you are working for your demise.

Is that a ***Greek Fatality*** curse? It is a law of nature, a balance in the order of things. That does not mean that you should stop what you are doing. You are just part of the equation, you still have to deliver your part and to walk your **Destiny**. That said, if you know what is coming ahead, is there any way for you the leverage that knowledge?

If your rival is shaping from your actions and their consequences, help yourself by acknowledging the collaterals that you are leaving behind. The fewer the collaterals, the fewer the risks to have a rival rising quickly from your actions.

If your rise was from empowering the others as I am teaching you, well, you will have much more love and allies than hate. About hate, look in the eyes of the jealous heart to understand where will the next strike come from.

But those are not the real rivals that will take you down unless you've grown cocky and lost your edge. They are not strong enough to defeat the wave that they surfed themselves.

Your real demise will come from those who have suffered your actions and who have paid dearly their consequences. That will be your demise because you have a blind angle.

This will happen to every power making a difference. Unless we replace the word power with something else... influence perhaps?

A ***Greek Fatality*** is by definition something that cannot be avoided. Well, that's wording and culture, that's part of Conformity and of our legacy. Well, here is my challenge to you, can you change the world, doing better than those who preceded us?

I am taking that challenge with 3 words, **VISION**, **COMPASSION**, and **COLLABORATION**. What are yours?

This is **Shortcut volume 3, LEADERSHIP**. Welcome to the Alphas.

PART 8

"FAMOUS QUOTES"

by Dr. BAK NGUYEN

0001

FROM SYMPHONY OF SKILLS

"The pain of the problem has to be greater than the pain of change."

Dr. Bak Nguyen

0002

FROM SYMPHONY OF SKILLS

"Sharing is the way to grow."

Dr. Bak Nguyen

0003

FROM LEADERSHIP, PANDORA'S BOX

"One's legend can only begin the day one's Quest of Identity is over."

Dr. Bak Nguyen

0004

FROM IDENTITY, ANTHOLOGY OF QUESTS

"Gratitude is the only past with a future."

Dr. Bak Nguyen

0005

FROM PROFESSION HEALTH

"Mine was, forgive yourself."

Dr. Bak Nguyen

0006

FROM INDUSTRIES' DISRUPTORS

"To walk on thin ice is a dangerous game.
To run is safer. To surf is the easiest."

Dr. Bak Nguyen

0007

FROM INDUSTRIES' DISRUPTORS

"If I have changed the world from a dental chair,
you are all in a better position than I am
to change the world."

Dr. Bak Nguyen

0008

FROM INDUSTRIES' DISRUPTORS

"The day you are fighting to raise the average instead of beating it, that day, you've joined the leadership."

Dr. Bak Nguyen

0009

FROM INDUSTRIES' DISRUPTORS

"At the end of the day, business is communication."

Dr. Bak Nguyen

0010

FROM INDUSTRIES' DISRUPTORS

"Make leverage of each of your liabilities, and you will always be moving forward."

Dr. Bak Nguyen

0011

FROM INDUSTRIES' DISRUPTORS

"I believe in myself and I do it for God, not the other way around."

Dr. Bak Nguyen

0012

FROM INDUSTRIES' DISRUPTORS

"Always choose the path of least resistance."

Dr. Bak Nguyen

0013

FROM INDUSTRIES' DISRUPTORS

"Be mindful of the consequences."

Dr. Bak Nguyen

0014

FROM CHANGING THE WORLD FROM A DENTAL CHAIR

"Hammering air three times over and it will become steel."

Dr. Bak Nguyen

0015

FROM CHANGING THE WORLD FROM A DENTAL CHAIR

"Mdex, for joy for life."

Dr. Bak Nguyen

0016

FROM CHANGING THE WORLD FROM A DENTAL CHAIR

"Confidence is sexy."

Dr. Bak Nguyen

0017

FROM CHANGING THE WORLD FROM A DENTAL CHAIR

"Make it happen!"

Dr. Bak Nguyen

0018

FROM THE POWER BEHIND THE ALPHA

"Humility is to know what you are and to recognize what you are not."

Dr. Bak Nguyen

0019

FROM MOMENTUM TRANSFER

"On thin ice, speed up, that's how you will eventually learn to fly! "

Dr. Bak Nguyen

0020

FROM MOMENTUM TRANSFER

"Control with wisdom is called influence."

Dr. Bak Nguyen

0021

FROM MOMENTUM TRANSFER

"To stabilize a momentum, speed up!"

Dr. Bak Nguyen

0022

FROM HYBRID

"Chords and patterns are the themes of the Universe."

Dr. Bak Nguyen

0023

FROM HYBRID

"A weakness is a strength out of reach."

Dr. Bak Nguyen

0024

FROM HYBRID

"Look for your next immediate win."

Dr. Bak Nguyen

0025

FROM REBOOT, TO GROW FROM MIDLIFE CRISIS

"Don't stop the flow of a river unless you are ready to clean up the flood."

Dr. Bak Nguyen

0026

FROM LEVERAGE COMMUNICATION INTO SUCCESS

"Find your worth in the service of others."

Dr. Bak Nguyen

0027

FROM LEVERAGE COMMUNICATION INTO SUCCESS

"Humility is not the denial of oneself but the acceptance of one true nature."

Dr. Bak Nguyen

0028

FROM THE BOOK OF LEGENDS, VOLUME 1

"We are all born little, as a chicken heart. If we keep an open mind, we will grow into a lion heart. Some will choose to be close-minded and will remain small."

Dr. Bak Nguyen

0029

FROM THE BOOK OF LEGENDS, VOLUME 1

"To have an open mind is step one.
To keep growing, one needs an open heart."

Dr. Bak Nguyen

0030

FROM THE BOOK OF LEGENDS, VOLUME 1

"Humility is the ability to recognize and to respect what we are, and stop pretending to be what we are not."

Dr. Bak Nguyen

0031

FROM SELFMADE

"Good things start to happen when you say yes!"

Dr. Bak Nguyen

0032

FROM SELFMADE

"Knowledge is the ground of the past.
Hope and Dreams are the air of the future."

Dr. Bak Nguyen

0033

FROM SELFMADE

"My deepest fear is to show up before God and not have enough to show for."

Dr. Bak Nguyen

0034

FROM THE RISE OF THE UNICORN

"To make the world a better place."

Dr. Bak Nguyen

0035

FROM THE RISE OF THE UNICORN

"A Momentum is when it is easier
to keep moving than to stop."

Dr. Bak Nguyen

0036

FROM CHAMPION MINDSET

"I was open, and I bet on myself."

Dr. Bak Nguyen

0037

FROM HOW TO WRITE A BOOK IN 30 DAYS

"To keep Momentum, aim for the next win,
as little as it might be."

Dr. Bak Nguyen

0038

FROM HOW TO WRITE A BOOK IN 30 DAYS

"A quote is a truth from another life,
from a past legacy."

Dr. Bak Nguyen

0039

FROM HOW TO WRITE A BOOK IN 30 DAYS

"The fewer the words, the better."

Dr. Bak Nguyen

0040

FROM POWER, EMOTIONAL INTELLIGENCE

"Align your emotions and your ambitions to be whole, to be unstoppable."

Dr. Bak Nguyen

0041

FROM POWER, EMOTIONAL INTELLIGENCE

"I believe in myself, and I do it for God, not the other way around."

Dr. Bak Nguyen

0042

FROM BRANDING

"I kept the "Dr." on to remind me to always put your interests before mine."

Dr. Bak Nguyen

0043

FROM BRANDING

"Arrogance is not the bragging of our knowledge, but rather the denial of our ignorance."

Dr. Bak Nguyen

0044

FROM HORIZON VOLUME ONE

"I treat people, not teeth."

Dr. Bak Nguyen

0045

FROM THE POWER OF YES, VOLUME 1

"Writing books allowed me to evolve
at the speed of my thoughts."

Dr. Bak Nguyen

0046

FROM THE POWER OF YES, VOLUME 1

"Speed is my power. Momentum, my expression."

Dr. Bak Nguyen

0047

FROM THE POWER OF YES VOLUME 3

"We do not need to choose, only to prioritize."

Dr. Bak Nguyen

0048

FROM HOW TO NOT FAIL AS A DENTIST

"Changing the world from a dental chair."

Dr. Bak Nguyen

0049

FROM HOW TO NOT FAIL AS A DENTIST

"I am not giving up, I am simply wising up!"

Dr. Bak Nguyen

0050

FROM HOW TO NOT FAIL AS A DENTIST

"With your money, do not trust anyone but yourself."

Dr. Bak Nguyen

0051

FROM HUMILITY FOR SUCCESS

"Reading will be cool again!"

Dr. Bak Nguyen

0052

FROM HUMILITY FOR SUCCESS

"Until it is done, it is air, good air but only air."

Dr. Bak Nguyen

0053

FROM MASTERMIND

"You can cheat, legally, by learning about shortcuts and leveraging."

Dr. Bak Nguyen

0054

FROM PLAYBOOK INTRODUCTION VOLUME 1

"Nothing will last forever, and nothing is free."

Dr. Bak Nguyen

0055

FROM PLAYBOOK INTRODUCTION VOLUME 2

"Be careful since doubts is a pet
that you are feeding."

Dr. Bak Nguyen

0056

FROM PLAYBOOK INTRODUCTION VOLUME 2

"Reach for your next win as soon as possible,
and build on it!"

Dr. Bak Nguyen

0057

FROM AMONGST THE ALPHAS, VOLUME 2

"Be bold, confident, and humble."

Dr. Bak Nguyen

0058

FROM AMONGST THE ALPHAS, VOLUME 2

"Growth happens at the giving end,
not the receiving one."

Dr. Bak Nguyen

0059

FROM SUCCESS IS A CHOICE

"Be bold, be flexible, act fast and stay humble."

Dr. Bak Nguyen

0060

FROM SUCCESS IS A CHOICE

"To succeed, be flexible."

Dr. Bak Nguyen

0061

FROM 90 DAYS CHALLENGE

"In times of crisis, one has to reinvent oneself."

Dr. Bak Nguyen

0062

FROM RISING

"To matter, serve."

Dr. Bak Nguyen

0063

FROM RISING

"There is no free money."

Dr. Bak Nguyen

0064

FROM AFTERMATH

"For the first time of our lifetime,
all the interests of the world are aligned."

Dr. Bak Nguyen

0065

FROM AFTERMATH

"In times of crisis, it is the perfect opportunity to reinvent who we are. "

Dr. Bak Nguyen

0066

FROM AFTERMATH

"Yes, we can have it all!"

Dr. Bak Nguyen

0067

FROM TORNADO

"History will say that to celebrate one world record, we scored two more!"

Dr. Bak Nguyen

0068

FROM TORNADO

"The only way to keep overdelivering is playing, all-in!"

Dr. Bak Nguyen

0069

FROM TORNADO

"Dream and the means will come."

Dr. Bak Nguyen

0070

FROM ALPHA LADDERS VOLUME ONE

"All good things start with a YES."

Dr. Bak Nguyen

0071

FROM ALPHA LADDERS VOLUME 2

"Growth occurs at the giving end, always."

Dr. Bak Nguyen

0072

FROM THE CONFESSION OF AN OVERACHIEVER

"Being lazy doesn't mean that you don't have to do shit, it means that you don't have to go through shit to get things done."

Dr. Bak Nguyen

0073

FROM TO OVERACHIEVER EVERYTHING BEING LAZY

"Arrogance is not the recognition of who we are but the denial of what we are not."

Dr. Bak Nguyen

0074

FROM TO OVERACHIEVER EVERYTHING BEING LAZY

"You call me doctor to remind me to always put your needs before mine."

Dr. Bak Nguyen

0075

FROM TO OVERACHIEVER EVERYTHING BEING LAZY

"Nowadays, influence is power without liability."

Dr. Bak Nguyen

0076

FROM TO OVERACHIEVER EVERYTHING BEING LAZY

"I told you that everything in life is a trade. Be careful of what you are trading."

Dr. Bak Nguyen

0077

FROM SHORTCUT VOLUME 1 - HEALING

"Fear is a disease and it must be treated like one."

Dr. Bak Nguyen

This is **Shortcut volume 3, LEADERSHIP**. Welcome to the Alphas.

If I have changed the world from a dental chair,
you are all in a better position to change the world than I am.

Dr. BAK NGUYEN

CONCLUSION

by Dr. BAK NGUYEN

This is surely one of the most intense journeys that I have undertaken so far, the **SHORTCUT series**, but this volume, in particular, the first one of **RISING**, **LEADERSHIP**. Writing the last one, I lost a dear friend of mine. That reminded me of the fragility of life and of the value of Time as our most precious resource.

That's also why I have started the **RISING** series with **LEADERSHIP** instead of **CONFIDENCE**. If confidence is required to access leadership, I wrote just like there was no tomorrow and that it would be my last book, just to remind me of the importance of Time and of making the most of each day. If this was the end, I will have left a trilogy complete and worth your time.

That said, I am fortunate that this is just the end of this chapter, of **SHORTCUT volume 3, LEADERSHIP**, not the end of my journey. The next landmark ending will be the completion of my 100th book, in a month. There is still a long way before that one, before the world record and the celebrations. But unless God is eager to have back the talents he gave me and his profits, I still have much to do, writing a book every 4 days to deliver on this one.

This is my journey, my story. Yours is happening in parallel. If somehow **SHORTCUT LEADERSHIP** has helped you find inspiration to ease your way, I am glad that I have helped. Not just you, but all of those you will be helping. And that's the **Power of Influence**.

If you are following my logic, I am not sharing because I am noble, selfless, and anyhow better than any of you. I have shared because that's those are the talents that I've received from God.

I can run my own course, and I am doing that too. But through empowerment, helping each of you to reach your legend, that's is my way to fuck and cheat Time in the race, my greatest rival, since the good and ripple effect of your actions will also be part of my ledger as I have to stand in front of God.

Now that my motives are clear, what are yours? What is next for you and how are you yielding your powers? You don't have powers, no problem, they are laying ahead in the path of your legend. To find them, you must awake and dive headfirst.

I am glad that I had the privilege to share with you and to be part of your rise. Dr. Kien Quan Diec, one of my dearest mentors, thanked me after he taught me the art of leveraging options and the stock market. I was surprised and immediately responded that I was the one thanking him.

Today, I understand his feelings and what he meant by thanking me. I was going the keep his legacy going and hopefully, push it to the next level. Well, I thank each and every one of you to have taken the time to sit down with me. You are my hopes and leverage for a legacy. You are the allies who will testify for me as I will stand, one day, in front of God.

That said, I am not counting on you but on myself to respond to God's expectations. I will keep delivering and overdelivering until I run out of time, and even then!

This is my legend. What is yours?

This is **Shortcut volume 3, LEADERSHIP**. Welcome to the Alphas.

If I have changed the world from a dental chair,
you are all in a better position to change the world than I am.
Dr. BAK NGUYEN

ANNEX

GLOSSARY OF Dr. BAK's LIBRARY

1

1SELF -080

REINVENT YOURSELF FROM ANY CRISIS

BY Dr. BAK NGUYEN

In 1SELF is about to reinvent yourself to rise from any crisis. Written in the midst of the COVID war, now more than ever, we need hope and the know-how to bridge the future. More than just the journey of Dr. Bak, this time, Dr. Bak is sharing his journey with mentors and people who built part of the world as we know it. Interviewed in this book, CHRISTIAN TRUDEAU, former CEO and FOUNDER of BCE EMERGIS (BELL CANADA), he also digitalized the Montreal Stock Exchange.RON KLEIN, American Innovator, inventor of the magnetic stripe of the credit card, of MLS (Multi-listing services) and the man who digitalized WALL STREET bonds markets.ANDRE CHATELAIN, former first vice-president of the MOVEMENT DESJARDINS. Dr. JEAN DE SERRES, former CEO of HEMA QUEBEC. These men created billions in values and have changed our lives, even without us knowing. They all come together to share their experiences and knowledge to empower each and everyone to emerge stronger from this crisis, from any crisis.

AFTERMATH -063

BUSINESS AFTER THE GREAT PAUSE

BY Dr. BAK NGUYEN & Dr. ERIC LACOSTE

In AFTERMATH, Dr. Bak joins forces with Community leader and philanthrope Dr. Eric Lacoste. Two powerful minds and forces of nature in the reaction to the worst economic meltdown in modern times. We are all victims of the CORONA virus. Both just like humans have learned to adapt to survive, so is our economy. Most business structures and management philosophies are inherited from the age of industrialization and beyond. COVID-19 has shot down the world economy with months. At the time of the AFTERMATH, the truth is many corporations and organizations will either have to upgrade to the INFORMATION AGE or disappear. More than the INFORMATION upgrade, the era of SOCIAL MEDIA and the MILLENNIALS are driving a revolution in the core philosophy of all organizations. Profit is not king anymore, support is. In this time and age where a teenager with a social account can compete with the million dollars PR firm, social implication is now the new cornerstone. Those who will adapt will prevail and prosper, while the resistance and old guards will soon be forgotten as fossils of a past era.

ALPHA LADDERS -075

CAPTAIN OF YOUR DESTINY

BY Dr. BAK NGUYEN & JONAS DIOP

In ALPHA LADDERS, Dr. Bak is sharing his private conversation and board meetings with 2 of his trusted lieutenants, strategist Jonas Diop and international Counsellor, Brenda Garcia. As both the Dr. Bak and ALPHA brands are gaining in popularity and traction, it was time to get the movement to the next level. Now, it's about building a community and to help everyone willing to become ALPHAS to find their powers. Dr. Bak is a natural recruiter of ALPHAS and peers. He also spent the last 20 years plus, training and mentoring proteges. Now comes the time to empower more and more proteges to become ALPHAS. ALPHAS LADDERS is the journey of how Dr. Bak went from a product of Conformity to rise into a force of Nature, know as a kind tornado. In ALPHA LADDERS Jonas pushed Dr. Bak to retrace each of the steps of his awakening, steps that we can breakdown and reproduce for ourselves. The goal is to empower each willing individual to become the ultimate Captain of his or her destiny, and to do it, again and again. Welcome to the Alphas.

ALPHA LADDERS 2 -081

SHAPING LEADERS AND ACHIEVERS

BY Dr. BAK NGUYEN & BRENDA GARCIA

In ALPHA LADDERS 2, Dr. Bak is sharing the second part of his private conversation and board meetings with his trusted lieutenants. This time it is with international Counsellor, Brenda Garcia that the dialogue is taking place. In this second tome, the journey is taken to the next level. If the first tome was about the WHYs and the HOWs at an individual level, this tome is about the WHYs and the HOWs at the societal level. Through the lens of her background in international relations and diplomacy, Brenda now has the mission to help Dr. Bak establish structures, not only for his emerging organization and legacy, THE ALPHAS, but to also inspire all the other leaders and structures of our society. To do this, Brenda is taking Dr. Bak on an anthropological, sociological and philosophical journey to revisit different historical key moments in various fields and eras, going as far back as in ancient Greece at the dawn of democracy, all the way to the golden era of modern multilateralism embodied by the UN structure. Learning from the legacies of prominent figures going from Plato to Ban Ki Moon, Martin Luther King or Nelson Mandela, to Machiavelli, Marx and Simone de Beauvoir, Brenda and Dr. Bak are attempting to grasp the essence of structure and hierarchy, their goal being to empower each willing individual to become the ultimate Captain of their own success, to climb up the ladders no matter how high it is, and to build their legacy one step at a time.

AMONGST THE ALPHAS -058

BY Dr. BAK NGUYEN, with Dr. MARIA KUNDSTATER, Dr. PAUL OUELLETTE and Dr. JEREMY KRELL

In AMONGST THE ALPHAS Dr. Bak opens the blueprint of the next level with the hope that everyone can be better, bigger, wiser, but above all, a philosophy of Life that if, well applied, can bring inspiration to life. The Alphas rose in the midst of the COVID war as an International Collaboration to empower individuals to rise from the global crisis. Joining Dr. Bak are some of the world thinkers and achievers, the Alphas. Doctors, business people, thinkers, achievers, influencers, they are coming together to define what is an Alpha and his or her role, making the world a better place. This isn't the American dream, it is the human dream, one that can help you make History.Joining Dr. Bak are 3 Alpha authors, Dr. Maria Kundstater, Dr. Paul Ouellette and Dr. Jeremy Krell. This book started with questions from coach Jonas Diop. Welcome to the Alphas.

AMONGST THE ALPHAS vol.2 -059

ON THE OTHER SIDE

BY Dr. BAK NGUYEN with Dr. JULIO REYNAFARJE, Dr. LINA DUSEVICIUTE and Dr. DUC-MINH LAM-DO

In AMONGST THE ALPHAS 2, Dr. Bak continues to explore the meaning of what it is to be an Alpha and how to act amongst Alphas, because as the saying taught us: alone one goes fast, together we goes far. Some people see the problem. Some people look at the problem, some people created the problem. Some people leverage the problem into solutions and opportunities. Well, all of those people are Alphas. Networking and leveraging one another, their powers and reach are beyond measure. And one will keep the other in line too. Joining Dr. Bak are 3 Alphas from around the world coming together to share and collaborate, Dr. DUSEVICIUTE, Dr. LAM-DO and Dr. REYNAFARJE. This isn't the American dream, it is the human dream, one that can help you make History. Welcome to the Alphas.

BOOTCAMP -071

BOOKS TO REWRITE MINDSETS INTO WINNING STATES OF MIND

BY Dr. BAK NGUYEN

In BOOTCAMP 8 BOOKS TO REWRITE MINDSETS INTO WINNING STATES OF MIND, Dr. Bak is taking you into his past, before the visionary entrepreneur, before the world records, before the Industry's disruptor status. Here are 8 of the books that changed Dr. Bak's thinking and, therefore, reset his evolution into the course we now know him for. BOOTCAMP: 8 BOOKS TO REWRITE MINDSETS INTO WINNING STATES OF MIND, is a Bootcamp of 8 weeks for anyone looking to experience Dr. Bak's training to become THE Dr. BAK you came to know and love. This book will summarize how each title changed Dr. Bak mindset into a state of mind and how he applied that to rewrite his destiny. 8 books to read, that's 8 weeks of Bootcamp to access the power of your MIND and of your WILL. Are you ready for a change?

BRANDING -044

BALANCING STRATEGY AND EMOTIONS

BY Dr. BAK NGUYEN

BRANDING is communication to its most powerful state. Branding is not just about communicating anymore but about making a promise, about establishing a relation, about generating an emotion. More than once, Dr. Bak proved himself to be a master, communicating and branding his ideas into flags attracting interest and influences, nationally and internationally. In BRANDING, Dr. Bak shares a very unique and personal journey, branding Dr. Bak. How does he go from Dr. Nguyen, a loved and respected dentist to becoming Dr. Bak, a world anchor hosting THE ALPHAS in the medical and financial world?More than a personal journey, BRANDING helps to break down the steps to elevate someone with nothing else but the force of his or her spirit. Welcome to the Alphas.

CHANGING THE WORLD FROM A DENTAL CHAIR -007

BY Dr. BAK NGUYEN

Since he has received the EY's nomination for entrepreneur of the year for his startup Mdex & Co, Dr. Bak Nguyen has pushed the opportunity to the next level. Speaker, author, and businessman, Dr. Bak is a true entrepreneur and industries' disruptor. To compensate for the startup's status of Mdex & Co, he challenged himself to write a book based on the EY's questionnaire to share an in-depth vision of his company. With "Changing the World from a dental chair" Dr. Bak is sharing his thought process and philosophy to his approach to the industry. Not looking to revolutionize but rather to empower, he became, despite himself, an industries disruptor: an entrepreneur who has established a new benchmark. Dr. Bak Nguyen is a cosmetic dentist and visionary businessman who won the GRAND HOMAGE prize of "LYS de la Diversité" 2016, for his contribution as a citizen and entrepreneur in the community. He also holds recognitions from the Canadian Parliament and the Canadian Senate.

In 2003, he founded Mdex, a dental company upon which in 2018, he launched the most ambitious private endeavour to reform the dental industry, Canada wide. He wrote seven books covering ENTREPRENEURSHIP, LEADERSHIP, QUEST of IDENTITY, and now, PROFESSION HEALTH. Philosopher, he has close to his heart the quest of happiness of the people surrounding him, patients, and colleagues alike. Those projects have allowed Dr. Nguyen to attract interests from the international and diplomatic community and he is now the centre of a global discussion on the wellbeing and the future of the health profession. It is in that matter that he shares with you his thoughts and encourages the health community to share their own stories.

CHAMPION MINDSET -039

LEARNING TO WIN

BY Dr. BAK NGUYEN & CHRISTOPHE MULUMBA

CHAMPION MINDSET is the encounter of the business world and the professional sports world. Industries' Disruptor Dr. BAK NGUYEN shares his wisdom and views with the HAMMER, CFL Football Star, Edmonton's Eskimos CHRISTOPHE MULUMBA on how to leverage on the champion mindset to create successful entrepreneurs. Writing and challenging each other, they discovered the parallels and the difference of both worlds, but mainly, the recipe for leveraging from one to succeed in the other, from champions and entrepreneurs to WINNERS. Build and score your millions, it is a matter of mindset! This is CHAMPION MINDSET.

EMPOWERMENT -069

BY Dr. BAK NGUYEN

In EMPOWERMENT, Dr. Bak's 69th book, writing a book every 8 days for 8 weeks in a row to write the next world record of writing 72 books/36 months, Dr. Bak is taking a rest, sharing his inner feelings, inspiration, and motivation. Much more than his dairy, EMPOWERMENT is the key to walk in his footsteps and to comprehend the process of an overachiever. Dr. Bak's helped and inspired countless people to find their voice, to live their dream, and to be the better version of themselves. Why is he sharing as much and keep sharing? Why is he going that fast, always further and further, why and how is he keeping his inspiration and momentum? Those are all the answers EMPOWERMENT will deliver to you. This book might be one of the fastest Dr. Bak has written, not because of time constraints but from inspiration, pure inspiration to share and to grow. There is always a dark side to each power, two faces to a coin. Well, this is the less prominent facets of Dr. Bak Momentum and success, the road to his MINDSET.

FORCES OF NATURE -015
FORGING THE CHARACTER OF WINNERS
BY Dr. BAK NGUYEN

In FORCES OF NATURE, Dr. Bak is giving his all. This is his 15 books written within 15 months. It is the end of a marathon to set the next world record. For the occasion, he wanted to end with a big bang! How about a book with all of his biggest challenges? A Quest of Identity, a journey looking for his name and powers, Dr. Bak is borrowing with myths and legends to make this journey universal. Yes, this is Dr. Bak's mythology. Demons, heroes and Gods, there are forces of Nature that we all meet on our way for our name. Some will scare us, some will fight us, some will manipulate us. We can flee, we can hide, we can fight. What we do will define our next encounter and the one after. A tale of personal growth, a journey to find power and purpose, Dr. Bak is showing us the path to freedom, the Path of Life. Welcome to the Alphas.

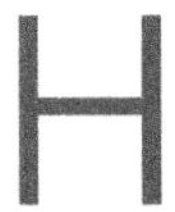

HORIZON, BUILDING UP THE VISION -045
VOLUME ONE
BY Dr. BAK NGUYEN

Dr. Bak is opening up at your demand! Many of you are following Dr. Bak online and are asking to know more about his lifestyle. This is how he has chosen to respond: sharing his lifestyle as he traveled the world and what he learned in each city to come to build his Mindset as a driver and a winner. Here are 10 destinations (over 69 that will be following in the next volumes...) in which he shares his journey. New York, Quebec, Paris, Punta Cana, Monaco, Los Angeles, Nice, Holguin, the journey happened over twenty years.

HORIZON, ON THE FOOTSTEP OF TITANS -048

VOLUME TWO

BY Dr. BAK NGUYEN

Dr. Bak is opening up at your demand! Many of you are following Dr. Bak online and are asking to know more about his lifestyle. This is how he has chosen to respond: sharing his lifestyle as he traveled the world and what he learned in each city to come to build his Mindset as a driver and a winner. Here are 9 destinations (over 72 that will be following in the next volumes...) in which he shares his journey. Hong Kong, London, Rome, San Francisco, Anaheim, and more..., the journey happened over twenty years. Dr. Bak is sharing with you his feelings, impressions, and how they shaped his state of mind and character into Dr. Bak. From a dreamer to a driver and a builder, the journey started since he was 3. Wealth is a state of mind, and a state of mind is the basis of the drive. Find out about the mind of an Industry's disruptor.

HORIZON, Dr.EAMING OF THE FUTURE -068

VOLUME THREE

BY Dr. BAK NGUYEN

Dr. Bak is back. From the midst of confinement, he remembers and writes about what life was, when traveling was a natural part of Life. It will come back. Now more than ever, we need to open both our hearts and minds to fight fear and intolerance. Writing from a time of crisis, he is sharing the magic and psychological effect of seeing the world and how it has shaped his mindset. Here are 9 other destinations (over 75) in which he shares his journey. Beijing, Key West, Madrid, Amsterdam, Marrakech and more..., the journey happened over twenty years.

HOW TO NOT FAIL AS A DENTIST -047

BY Dr. BAK NGUYEN

In HOW TO NOT FAIL AS A DENTIST, Dr. Bak is given 20 plus years of experience and knowledge of what it is to be a dentist on the ground. PROFESSIONAL INTELLIGENCE, FINANCIAL INTELLIGENCE and MANAGEMENT INTELLIGENCE are the fields that any dentist will have to master for a chance to success and a shot for happiness practicing dentistry. Where ever you are starting your career as a new graduate or a veteran in the field looking to reach the next level, this is book smart and street smart all into one. This is Million Dollar Mindset applied to dentistry. We won't be making a millionaire out of you from this book, we will be giving you a shot to happiness and success. The million will follow soon enough.

HOW TO WRITE A BOOK IN 30 DAYS -042

BY Dr. BAK NGUYEN

In HOW TO WRITE YOUR BOOK IN 30 DAYS, Dr. Bak has crafted writing skills and techniques that can be shared and mastered. This book is mainly about structure and how to keep moving forward, avoiding the hit of the INSPIRATION WALL. You will find a wealth of wisdom from his experience writing your first, second, or even 10th book. Dr. Bak is sharing his secrets writing books, having written himself 72 books within 36 months. Visionary businessman, doctor in dentistry, Dr. Bak describes himself as a Dentist by circumstances, a communicator by passion, and an entrepreneur by nature.

HOW TO WRITE A SUCCESSFUL BUSINESS PLAN -049

BY Dr. BAK NGUYEN & ROUBA SAKR

In HOW TO WRITE A SUCCESSFUL BUSINESS PLAN, Dr. Bak is given 20 plus years of experience and knowledge of what it is to be an entrepreneur and more importantly, how to have the investors and banks on your side. Being an entrepreneur is surely not something you learn from school, but there are steps to master so you can communicate your views and vision. That's the only way you will have financing.Writing a business is only not a mandatory stop only for the bankers, but an essential step to every entrepreneur, to know the direction and what's coming next. A business plan is also not set in stone, if there is a truth in business is that nothing will go as planned. Writing down your business plan the first time will prepare you to adapt and to overcome the challenges and surprises. For most entrepreneurs, a business is a passion. To most investors and all banks, a business is a system. Your business plan is the map to that system. However unique your ideas and business are, the mapping follows the same steps and pattern.

HUMILITY FOR SUCCESS -051

BALANCING STRATEGY AND EMOTIONS

BY Dr. BAK NGUYEN

HUMILITY FOR SUCCESS is exploring the emotional discomforts and challenges champions, and overachievers put themselves through. Success is never done overnight and on the way, just like the pain and the struggles aren't enough, we are dealing with the doubts, the haters, and those who like to tell us how to live our lives and what to do. At the same time, nothing of worth can be achieved alone. Every legend has a cast of characters, allies, mentors, companions, rivals, and foes. So one needs the key to social behaviour. HUMILITY FOR SUCCESS is exploring the matter and will help you sort out beliefs from values, peers from friends. Humility is much more about how we see ourselves than how others see us. For any entrepreneur and champion, our daily is to set our mindset right, and to perfect our skills, not to fit in. There is a world where CONFIDENCE grows is in synergy with HUMILITY. As you set the right label on the right belief, you will be able to grow and to leave the lies and haters far behinds. This is HUMILITY FOR SUCCESS.

HYBRID -011

THE MODERN QUEST OF IDENTITY

BY Dr. BAK NGUYEN

I

IDENTITY -004

THE ANTHOLOGY OF QUESTS

BY Dr. BAK NGUYEN

What if John Lennon was still alive and running for president today? What kind of campaign will he be running? IDENTIFY -THE ANTHOLOGY OF QUESTS is about the quest each of us has to undertake, sooner or later, THE QUEST OF IDENTITY. Citizen of the world, aim to be one, the one, one whole, one unity, made of many. That's the anthology of life! Start with your one, find your unity, and your legend will start. We are all small-minded people anyway! We need each other to be one! We need each other to be happy, so we, so you, so I, can be happy. This is the chorus of life. This is our song! Citizens of the world, I salute you! This is the first tome of the IDENTITY QUEST. FORCES OF NATURE (tome 2) will be following in SUMMER 2021. Also under development, Tome 3 - THE CONQUEROR WITHIN will start production soon.

INDUSTRIES DISRUPTORS -006

BY Dr. BAK NGUYEN

INDUSTRIES DISRUPTORS is a strange title, one that sparkles mixed feelings. A disruptor is someone making a difference, and since we, in general, do not like change, the label is mostly negative. But a disruptor is mostly someone who sees the same problem and challenge from another angle. The disruptor will tackle that angle and come up with something new from something existent. That's evolution! In INDUSTRIES DISRUPTORS, Dr. Bak is joining forces with James Stephan-Usypchuk to share with us what is going on in the minds and shoes of those entrepreneurs disrupting the old habits. Dr. Bak is changing the world from a dental chair, disrupting the dental, and now the book industry. James is a maverick in the Intelligence space, from marketing to Artificial Intelligence. Coming from very different backgrounds and industries, they end up telling very similar stories. If disruptors change the world, well, their story proves that disruptors can be made and forged. Here's the recipe. Here are their stories.

KRYPTO -040
TO SAVE THE WORLD
BY Dr. BAK NGUYEN & ILYAS BAKOUCH

L

LEADERSHIP -003
PANDORA'S BOX
BY Dr. BAK NGUYEN

LEADERSHIP, PANDORA'S BOX is 21 presidential speeches for a better tomorrow for all of us. It aims to drive HOPE and motivation into each and every one of us. Together we can make the difference, we hold such power. Covering themes from LOYALTY to GENEROSITY, from FREEDOM and INTELLIGENCE to DOUBTS and DEATH, this is not the typical presidential or motivational speeches that we are used to. LEADERSHIP PANDORA'S BOX will surf your emotions first, only to dive with you to touch the core and soul of our meaning: to matter. This is not a Quest of Identity, but the cry to rally as a species, to raise our heads toward the future, and to move forward as a WHOLE. Not a typical Dr. Bak's book, LEADERSHIP, PANDORA'S BOX is a must-read for all of you looking for hope and purpose, all of us, citizens of the world.

LEVERAGE -014

COMMUNICATION INTO SUCCESS

BY Dr. BAK NGUYEN

In LEVERAGE COMMUNICATION TO SUCCESS, Dr. Bak shares his secret and mindsets to elevate an idea into a vision and a vision into an endeavour. Some endeavours will be a project, some others will become companies, and some will grow into a movement. It does not matter, each started with great communication.Communication is a very vast concept, education, sale, sharing, empowering, coaching, preaching, entertaining. Those are all different kinds of communication. The intent differs, the audiences vary, the messages are unique but the frame can be templated and mastered. In LEVERAGE COMMUNICATION TO SUCCESS, Dr. Bak is loyal to his core, sharing only what he knows best, what he has done himself. This book is dedicated to communicating successfully in business.

MASTERMIND, 7 WAYS INTO THE BIG LEAGUE -052

BY Dr. BAK NGUYEN & JONAS DIOP

MASTERMIND, 7 WAYS INTO THE BIG LEAGUE is the result of the encounter of business coach Jonas Diop and Dr. Bak. As a professional podcaster and someone always seeking the truth and ways to leverage success and performance, coach Jonas is putting Dr. Bak to the test, one that should reveal his secret to overachieve month after month, accumulating a new world record every month. Follow those two great minds as they push each other to surpass themselves, each in their own way and own style. MASTERMIND, 7 WAYS INTO THE BIG LEAGUE is more than a roadmap to success, it is a journey and a live testimony as you are turning the pages, one by one.

MIDAS TOUCH -065

POST-COVID DENTISTRY

BY Dr. BAK NGUYEN, Dr. JULIO REYNAFARJE AND Dr. PAUL OUELLETTE

MIDAS TOUCH, is the memoir of what happened in the ALPHAS SUMMIT in the midst of the GREAT PAUSE as great minds throughout the world in the dental field are coming together. As the time of competition is obsolete, the new era of collaboration is blooming. This is the 3rd book of the ALPHAS, after AFTERMATH and RELEVANCY, all written in the midst of confinement. Dr. Julio Reynafarje is bearing this initiative, to share with you the secret of a successful and lasting relationship with your patients, balancing science and psychology, kindness, and professionalism. He personally invited the ALPHAS to join as co-author, Dr. Paul Ouellette, and Dr.

Paul Dominique, and Dr. Bak.Together, they have more than 100 years of combined experience, wisdom, trade, skills, philosophy, and secrets to share with you to empower you in the rebuilding of the dental profession in the aftermath of COVID. RELEVANCY was about coming together and to rebuild the future. MIDAS TOUCH is about how to build, one treatment plan at a time, one story at a time, one smile at a time.

MINDSET ARMORY -050

BY Dr. BAK NGUYEN

MINDSET ARMORY is Dr. Bak's 49th book, days after he completed his world record of writing 48 books within 24 months, on top of being a CEO of Mdex & Co and a full-time cosmetic dentist. Dr. Bak is undoubtedly an OVERACHIEVER. From his last books, he has shared more and more of his lifestyle and how it forged his winning mindset. Within MINDSET ARMORY, Dr. Bak is sharing with us his tools, how he found them, forged them, and leverage them. Just like any warrior needs a shield, a sword, and a ride, here are Dr. Bak's. For any entrepreneur, the road to success is a long and winding journey. On the way, some will find allies and foes. Some allies will become foes, and some foes might become allies. In today's competitive world, the only constant is change. With the right tool, it is possible to achieve. The right tool, the right mindset. This is MINDSET ARMORY.

MIRROR-085

BY Dr. BAK NGUYEN

MIRROR is the theme for a personal book. Not only to Dr. Bak but to all of us looking to reach beyond who and what we actually are. MIRROR is special in the fact that it is not only the content of the book that is of worth but the process in which Dr. Bak shared his own evolution. To go beyond who we are, one must grow every day. And how do you compare your growth and how far have you reach? Looking in the mirror. In all of Dr. Bak's writing, looking at the past is a trap to avoid at all costs. Looking in the mirror, is that any better? Share Dr. Bak's way to push and keep pushing himself without friction nor resistance. Please read that again. To evolve without friction or resistance... that is the source of infinite growth and the unification of the Quest for Power and the Quest of Happiness.

MOMENTUM TRANSFER -009

BY Dr. BAK NGUYEN & Coach DINO MASSON

How to be successful in your business and in your life? Achieve Your Biggest Goals With MOMENTUM TRANSFER. START THE BUSINESS YOU WANT - AND BRING IT NEXT LEVEL! GET THE LIFE YOU ALWAYS WANTED - AND IMPROVE IT! TAKE ANY PROJECTS YOU HAVE - AND MAKE IT THE BEST! In this powerful book, you'll discover what a small business owner learned from a millionaire and successful entrepreneur. He applied his mentor's principles and is explaining them in full detail in this book. The small business owner wrote the book he has always wanted to read and went from the verge of bankruptcy to quadrupling his revenues in less than 9 months and improve his personal life by increasing his energy and bring back peacefulness. Together, the millionaire and the small business owner are sharing their most valuable business and life lessons to the world. The most powerful book to increase your momentum in your business and your life introduces simple and radical life-changing concepts: Multiply your business revenues by finding the Eye of your Momentum - Increase your energy by building and feeding your own Momentum - How to increase your confidence with these simple steps - How to transfer your new powerful energy into other aspects of your business and life - How to set goals and achieve them (even crush them!)- How to always tap into an effortless and limitless force within you- And much, much more!

PLAYBOOK INTRODUCTION -055

BY Dr. BAK NGUYEN

In PLAYBOOK INTRODUCTION, Dr. Bak is open the door to all the newcomers and aspirant entrepreneurs who are looking at where and when to start. Based on questions of two college students wanting to know how to start their entrepreneurial journey, Dr. Bak dives into his experiences to empower the next generation, not about what they should do, but how he, Dr. Bak, would have done it today. This is an important aspect to recognize in the business world, the world has changed since the INFORMATION AGE and the advent of the millenniums into the market. Most matrix and know-how have to be adapted to today's speed and accessibility to the information. We are living at the INFORMATION AGE, this book is the precursor to the ABUNDANCE AGE, at least to those open to embrace the opportunity.

PLAYBOOK INTRODUCTION 2 -056

BY Dr. BAK NGUYEN

In PLAYBOOK INTRODUCTION 2, Dr. Bak continuing the journey to welcome the newcomers and aspirant entrepreneurs looking at where and when to start. If the first volume covers the mindset, the second is covering much more in-depth the concept of debt and leverage.This is an important aspect to recognize in the business world, the world has changed since the INFORMATION AGE and the advent of the millenniums into the market. Most matrix and know-how have to be adapted to today's speed and accessibility to the information. We are living at the INFORMATION AGE, this book is the precursor to the ABUNDANCE AGE, at least to those open to embrace the opportunity.

POWER -043

EMOTIONAL INTELLIGENCE

BY Dr. BAK NGUYEN

IN POWER, EMOTIONAL INTELLIGENCE, Dr. Bak is sharing his experiences and secrets leveraging on his EMOTIONAL INTELLIGENCE, a power we all have within. From SYMPATHY, having others opening up to you, to ACTIVE LISTENING, saving you time and energy; from EMPATHY, allowing you to predict the future to INFLUENCE, enabling you to draft the future, not to forget the power of the crowd with MOMENTUM, you are now in possession of power in tune with nature, yourself. It is a unique take on the subject to empower you to find your powers and your destiny. Visionary businessman, doctor in dentistry, Dr. Bak describes himself as a Dentist by circumstances, a communicator by passion, and an entrepreneur by nature.

POWERPLAY -078
HOW TO BUILD THE PERFECT TEAM
BY Dr. BAK NGUYEN

In POWERPLAY, HOW TO BUILD THE PERFECT TEAM, Dr. Bak is sharing with you his experience, perspective, and mistake traveling the journey of the entrepreneur. A serial entrepreneur himself, he started venture only with a single partner as team to build companies with a director of human resources and a board of directors. POWERPLAY is not a story, it is the HOW TO build the perfect team, knowing that perfection is a lie. So how can one build a team that will empower his or her vision? How to recruit, how to train, how to retain? Those are all legitimate questions. And all of those won't matter if the first question isn't answered: what is the reason for the team? There is the old way to hire and the new way to recruit. Yes, Human Resources is all about mindset too! This journey is one of introspection, of leadership, and a cheat sheet to build, not only the perfect team but the team that will empower your legacy to the next level.

PROFESSION HEALTH - TOME ONE -005
THE UNCONVENTIONAL QUEST OF HAPPINESS
BY Dr. BAK NGUYEN, Dr. MIRJANA SINDOLIC, Dr. ROBERT DURAND AND COLLABORATORS

Why are health professionals burning out while they give the best of themselves to heal the world? Dr. Bak aims to break the curse of isolation that health professionals face and establish a conversation to start the healing process. PROFESSION HEALTH is the basis of an ongoing discussion and will also serve as an introduction to a study lead by Professor Robert Durand, DMD, MSc Science from University of Montreal, study co-financed by Mdex and the Federal Government of Canada. Co-writers are Dr. Mirjana Sindolic, Professor Robert Durand, Dr. Jean De Serres, MD and former President of Hema Quebec, Counsel-Minister Luis Maria Kalaff Sanchez, Dr. Miguel Angel Russo, MD, Banker Anthony Siggia, Banker Kyles Yves, and more...
This is the first Tome of three, dedicated to help "WHITE COATS" to heal and to find their happiness.

REBOOT -012
MIDLIFE CRISIS
BY Dr. BAK NGUYEN

MidLife Crisis is a common theme to each of us as we reach the threshold. As a man, as a woman, why is it that half of the marriages end up in recall? If anything else would have half those rates of failure, the lawsuits would be raining. Where are the flaws, the traps? Love is strong and pure, why is marriage not the reflection of that? All hard to ask questions with little or no answers. Dr. Bak is sharing his reflections and findings as he reached himself the WALL OF MARRIAGE. This is a matter that affects all of our lives. It is time for some answers.

RELEVANCY - TOME TWO -064

REINVENTING OURSELVES TO SURVIVE

BY Dr. BAK NGUYEN & Dr. PAUL OUELLETTE AND COLLABORATORS

THE GREAT PAUSE was a reboot of all the systems of society. Many outdated systems will not make it back. The Dental Industry is a needed one, it has laid on complacency for far too long. In an age where expertise is global and democratized and can be replaced with technologies and artificial intelligence, the REBOOT will force, not just an update, but an operating system replacement and a firmware upgrade.First, they saved their industry with THE ALPHAS INITIATIVE, sharing their knowledge and vision freely to all the world's dental industry. With the OUELLETTE INITIATIVE, they bought some time to all the dental clinics to resume and to adjust. The warning has been given, the clock is now ticking. who will prevail and prosper and who will be left behind, outdated and obsolete?

RISING -062

TO WIN MORE THAN YOU ARE AFRAID TO LOSE

BY Dr. BAK NGUYEN

In RISING, TO WIN MORE TAN YOU ARE AFRAID TO LOSE, Dr. Bak is breaking down the strategy to success to all, not only those wearing white coats and scrubs. More than his previous book (SUCCESS IS A CHOICE), this one is covering most of the aspects of getting to the next level, psychologically, socially, and financially. Rising is broken down into three key strategies: Financial Leverage - Compressing time - Always being in control. Presented by MILLION DOLLAR MINDSET, the book is covering more than the ways to create wealth, but also how to reach happiness and to live a life without regrets. Dr. Bak the CEO and founder of Mdex & Co, a company with the promise of reforming the whole dental industry for the better. He wrote more than 60 books within 30 months as he is sharing his experiences, secrets, and wisdom.

S

SELFMADE -036
GRATITUDE AND HUMILITY
BY Dr. BAK NGUYEN

This is the story of Dr. Bak, an artist who became a dentist, a dentist who became an Entrepreneur, an Entrepreneur who is seeking to save an entire industry.In his free time, Dr. Bak managed to write 37 books and is a contender to 3 world records to be confirmed. Businessman and visionary, his views and philosophy are ahead of our time. This is his 37th book. In SELFMADE, Dr. Bak is answering the questions most entrepreneurs want to know, the HOWTO and the secret recipes, not just to succeed, but to keep going no matter what! SELFMADE is the perfect read for any entrepreneurs, novices, and veterans.

SUCCESS IS A CHOICE -060
BLUEPRINTS FOR HEALTH PROFESSIONALS
BY Dr. BAK NGUYEN

In SUCCESS IS A CHOICE, FINANCIAL MILLIONAIRE BLUEPRINTS FOR HEALTH PROFESSIONALS, Dr. Bak is breaking down the strategy to success for all those wearing white coats and scrubs: doctors, dentists, pharmacists, chiropractors, nurses, etc. Success is broken down into three key strategies: Financial Leverage - Compressing time - Always being in control. Presented by MILLION DOLLAR MINDSET, the book is covering more than the ways to create wealth, but also how to reach happiness and to live a life without regrets.Dr. Bak is a successful cosmetic dentist with nearly 20 years of experience. He founded Mdex & Co, a company with the promise of reforming the whole dental industry for the better. While doing so, he discovered a passion for writing and for sharing. Multiple times World Record, Dr. Bak is writing a book every 2 weeks for the last 30 months. This is his 60th book, and he is still practicing. How he does it, is what he is sharing with us, SUCCESS, HAPPINESS, and mostly FREEDOM to all Health Professionals.

SYMPHONY OF SKILLS -001
BY Dr. BAK NGUYEN

You will enlighten the world with your potential. I can't wait to see all the differences that you will have in our world. Remember that power comes with responsibility. We can feel in his presence, a genuine force, a depth of energy, confidence, innocence, courage, and intelligence. Bak is always looking for answers, morning and night, he wants to understand the why and the why not. This book is the essence of the man. Dr. Bak is a force of nature who bears proudly his title eHappy. The man never ceases smiling nor spreading his good vibe wherever he passes. He is not trapped in the nostalgia of the past nor the satisfaction of the present, he embodies the joy of what's possible, what's to come. The more we read, the more we share, and we live. That is Bak, he charms us to evolve and to share his points of view, and before we know it, we are walking by his side, a journey we never saw coming.

T

THE 90 DAYS CHALLENGE -061

BY Dr. BAK NGUYEN

THE 90 DAYS CHALLENGE, is Dr. Bak's journey into the unknown. Overachiever writing 2 books a month on average, for the last 30 months, ambitious CEO, Industries' Disruptor, Dr. Bak seems to have success in everything he touches. Everything except the control of his weight. For nearly 20 years, he struggles with an overweight problem. Every time he scored big, he added on a little more weight. Well, this time, he exposes himself out there, in real-time and without filter, accepting the challenge of his brother-in-law, DON VO to lose 45 pounds within 90 days. That's half a pound a day, for three months. He will have to do so while keeping all of his other challenges on track, writing books at a world record pace, leading the dental industry into the new ERA, and keep seeing his patients. Undoubtedly entertaining, this is the journey of an ALPHA who simply won't give up. But this time, nothing is sure.

THE BOOK OF LEGENDS -024

BY Dr. BAK NGUYEN & WILLIAM BAK

The Book of Legends vol. 1 the story behind the world record of Dr. Bak and his son, William Bak. All Dr. Bak had in mind was to keep his promise of writing a book with his son. They ended up writing 8 children's books within a month, scoring a new world record. William is also the youngest author having published in two languages. Those are world records waiting to be confirmed. History will say: to celebrate a first world record (writing 15 books / 15 months), for the love of his son, he will have scored a second world record: to write 8 books within a month! THE BOOK OF LEGENDS vol. 1 This is both a magical journey for both a father and a son looking to connect and to find themselves. Join Dr. Bak and William Bak in their journey and their love for Life!

THE BOOK OF LEGENDS 2 -041

BY Dr. BAK NGUYEN & WILLIAM BAK

THE BOOK OF LEGENDS vol. 2 is the sequel of "CINDERELLA" but a true story between a father and his son. Together they have discovered a bond and a way to connect. The first BOOK OF LEGENDS covered the time of the first four books they wrote together within a month. The second BOOK OF LEGENDS is covering what happened after the curtains dropped, what happened after reality kicked back in. If the first volume was about a fairy tale in vacation time, the second volume is about making it last in real Life. Share their journey and their love of Life!

THE BOOK OF LEGENDS 3 -086

THE END OF THE INNOCENCE AGE

BY Dr. BAK NGUYEN & WILLIAM BAK

This is the third volume of the series, THE BOOK OF LEGENDS. If the first two happened as a breeze breaking world records on top of world records (27 books written as father and son), the 3rd volume took much more time to arrive. William has grown and writing chicken books is not enough anymore to ignite his imagination. Dr. Bak, as a good father, will try to follow William's growth and invented new games, technics and mind frames to keep engaging William's imagination and interest. From auditions to backstories, Dr. Bak bent backward to keep the adventure going. More than sharing the success and the glory, within THE BOOK OF LEGENDS volume 3, you are sharing the doubts and failure of a father and son refusing to let go... but who have now left MOMENTUM... until the winds blow once more in their favour. Welcome to the Alphas.

THE CONFESSION OF A LAZY OVERACHIEVER -089

REINVENT YOURSELF FROM ANY CRISIS

BY Dr. BAK NGUYEN

In THE CONFESSION OF A LAZY OVERACHIEVER, Dr. Bak is opening up to his new marketing officer, Jamie, fresh out of school. She is young, full of energy, and looking to chill and still to have it all. True to his character, Dr. Bak is giving Jamie some leeway to redefine Dr. Bak's brand to her demographic, the Millennials. This journey is about Dr. Bak satisfying the Millennials and answering their true questions in life. A rebel himself, his ambition to change the world started back on campus, some 25 years ago... then, life caught up with him. It took Dr. Bak 20 years to shake down the burdens of life, to spread his wings free from Conformity, and to start Overachieving. Doctor, CEO, and world record author, here is what Dr. Bak would have love to know 25 years ago as was still on campus. In a word, this is cheating your way to success and freedom. And yes, it is possible. Success, Money, Freedom, it all starts with a mindset and the awareness of Time. Welcome to the Alphas.

THE ENERGY FORMULA -053

BY Dr. BAK NGUYEN

THE ENERGY FORMULA is a book dedicated to help each individual to find the means to reach their purpose and goal in Life. Dr. Bak is a philosopher, a strategist, a business, an artist, and a dentist, how does he do all of that? He is doing so while mentoring proteges and leading the modernization of an entire industry. Until now, Momentum and Speed were the powers that he was building on and from. But those powers come from somewhere too. From a guide of our Quest of Identity, he became an ally in everyone's journey for happiness. THE ENERGY FORMULA is the book revealing step by step, the logic of building the right mindset and the way to ABUNDANCE and HAPPINESS, universally. It is not just a HOW TO book, but one that will change your life and guide you to the path of ABUNDANCE.

THE MODERN WOMAN -070

TO HAVE IT HAVE WITH NO SACRIFICE

BY Dr. BAK NGUYEN & Dr. EMILY LETRAN

In THE MODERN WOMAN: TO HAVE IT ALL WITH NO SACRIFICE, Dr. Bak joins forces with Dr. Emily Letran to empower all women to fulfill their desires, goals, and ambition. Both overachievers going against the odds, they are sharing their experience and wisdom to help all women to find confidence and support to redefine their lives. Dr. Emily Letran is a doctor in dentistry, an entrepreneur, author, and CERTIFIED HIGH-PERFORMANCE coach. For an Asian woman, she made it through the norms and the red tapes to find her voice. As she learned and grew with mentors, today she is sharing her secret with the energy that will motivate all of the female genders to stand for what they deserve. Alpha doctor, Bak is joining his voice and perspective since this is not about gender equality, but about personal empowerment and the quest of Identity of each, man and woman. Once more, Dr. Bak is bringing LEVERAGE and REASON to the new social deal between man and woman. This is not about gender, but about confidence.

THE POWER BEHIND THE ALPHA -008

BY TRANIE VO & Dr. BAK NGUYEN

It's been said by a "great man" that "We are born alone and we die alone." Both men and women proudly repeat those words as wisdom since. I apologize in advance, but what a fat LIE! That's what I learned and discovered in life since my mind and heart got liberated from the burden of scars and the ladders of society. I can have it all, not all at the same time, but I can have everything I put my mind and heart into. Actually, it is not completely true. I can have most of what I and Tranie put our minds into. Together, when we feel like one, there isn't much out of our reach. If I'm the mind, she's the heart; if I'm the Will, she's the means. Synergy is the core of our power.Tranie's aim is always Happiness. In Tranie's definition of life, there are no justifications, no excuses, no tomorrow. For Tranie, Happiness is measured by the minutes of every single day. This is why she's so strong and can heal people around her. That may also be why she doesn't need to talk much, since talking about the past or the future is, in her mind, dimming down the magic of the present, the Now. We both respect and appreciate that we are the whole balancing each other's equation of life, of love, of success. I was the plus and the minus, then I became the multiplication factor and grew into the exponential. And how is Tranie evolving in all of this? She is and always will be the balance. If anything, she is the equal sign of each equation.

THE POWER OF Dr. -066

THE MODERN TITLE OF NOBILITY

BY Dr. BAK NGUYEN, Dr. PAVEL KRASTEV AND COLLABORATORS

In THE POWER OF Dr., independent thinkers mean to exchange ideas. An idea can be very powerful if supported with a great work ethic. Work ethic, isn't that the main fabric of our white coats, scrubs, and title? In an era post-COVID where everything has been rebooted and that the healthcare industry is facing its own fate: to evolve or to be replaced, Dr. Bak and Dr. Pavel reveal the source of their power and their playbook to move forward, ahead.The power we all hold is our resilience and discipline. We put that for years at the service of our profession, from a surgical perspective. Now, we can harness that same power to rewrite the rules, the industry, and our future. Post-COVID, the rules are being rewritten, will you be part of the team or left behind?
"You can be in control!" More than personal growth and a motivational book, THE POWER OF Dr. is an awakening call to the doctor you look at when you graduate, with hope, with honour, with determination.

THE POWER OF YES -010

VOLUME ONE: IMPACT

BY Dr. BAK NGUYEN

In THE POWER OF YES, Dr. Bak is sharing his journey opening up and embracing the world, one day at a time, one ask at a time, one wish at a time. Far from a dare, saying YES allowed Dr. Bak to rewrite his mindsets and to break all the boundaries. This book is not one written a few days or weeks, but the accumulation of a journey for 12 months. The journeys started as Dr. Bak said YES to his producer to go on stage and to speak... That YES opened a world of possibilities. Dr. Bak embraced each and every one of them. 12 months later, he is celebrating the new world record of writing 9 books written over a period of 12 months. To him, it will be a miss, missing the 12 on 12 mark. To the rest of the world, they just saw the birth of a force of nature, the Alpha force. THE POWER OF YES is comprised of all the introduction of the adult books written by Dr. Bak within the first 12 months. Chapter by chapter, you can walk in his footstep seeing and smelling what he has. This is reality literature with a twist of POWER. THE POWER OF YES! Discover your potential and your power. This is the POWER OF YES, volume one. Welcome to the Alphas.

THE POWER OF YES 2 -037

VOLUME TWO: SHAPELESS

BY Dr. BAK NGUYEN

In THE POWER OF YES, volume 2, Dr. Bak is continuing his journey discovering his powers and influence. After 12 months embracing the world saying YES, he rose as an emerging force: he's been recognized as an INDUSTRIES DISRUPTOR, got nominated ERNST AND YOUNG ENTREPRENEUR OF THE YEAR, wrote 9 books within 12 months while launching the most ambitious private endeavour to reform his own industry, the dental field. Contender too many WORLD RECORDS, Dr. Bak is doing all of that in parallel. And yes, he is sleeping his nights and yes, he is writing his book himself, from the screen of his iPhone! Far from satisfied, Dr. Bak missed the mark of writing 12 books within 12 months and everything else is shaping and moving, and could come crumbling down at each turn. Now that Dr. Bak understands his powers, he is looking to test them and to push them to their limits, looking to keep scoring world records while materializing his vision and enterprises. This is the awakening of a Force of Nature looking to change the world for the better while having fun sharing. Welcome to the Alphas.

THE POWER OF YES 3 -046

VOLUME THREE: LIMITLESS

BY Dr. BAK NGUYEN

In THE POWER OF YES, volume 3, the journey of Dr. Bak continues where the last volume left, in front of 300 plus people showing up to his first solo event, a Dr. Bak's event. On stage and in this book, Dr. Bak reveals how 12 months saying YES to everything changed his life... actually, it was 18 months.
From a dentist looking to change the world from a dental chair into a multiple times world record author, the journey of openness is a rendez-vous with Fate. Dr. Bak is sharing almost in real-time his journey, experiences, but above all, his feelings, doubts, and comebacks. From one book to the next, from one journey to the next, follow the adventure of a man looking to find his name, his worth, and his place in the world. Doing so, he is touching people Doing so, he is touching people and initiating their rises. Are you ready for more? Are you ready to meet your Fate and Destiny? Welcome to the Alphas.

THE POWER OF YES 4 -087

VOLUME FOUR: PURPOSE

BY Dr. BAK NGUYEN

In THE POWER OF YES, volume 4, the journey continues days after where the last volume left. After setting the new world record of writing 48 books within 24 months, Dr. Bak is not ready to stop. As volume one covers 12 months of journey, volume 2 covers 6 months. Well, volume 3 covers 4 months. The speed is building up and increasing, steadily. This is volume 4, RISING, after breaking the sound barrier. Dr. Bak has reached a state where he is above most resistance and friction, he is now in a universe of his own, discovering his powers as he walks his journeys. This is no fiction story or wishful thinking, THE POWER OF YES is the journey of Dr. Bak, from one world record to the next, from one book to the next. You too can walk your own legend, you just need to listen to your innersole and to open up to the opportunity. May you get inspiration from the legendary journey of Dr. Bak and find your own Destiny. Welcome to the Alphas.

THE RISE OF THE UNICORN -038

BY Dr. BAK NGUYEN & Dr. JEAN DE SERRES

In THE RISE OF THE UNICORN, Dr. Bak is joining forces with his friend and mentor, Dr. Jean De Serres. Together both men had many achievements in their respective industries, but the advent of eHappyPedia, THE RISE OF THE UNICORN is a personal project dear to both of them: the QUEST OF HAPPINESS and its empowerment. This book is a special one since you are witnessing the conversation between two entrepreneurs looking to change the world by building unique tools and media. Just like any enterprise, the ride is never a smooth one in the park on a beautiful day. But this is about eHappyPedia, it is about happiness, right? So it will happen and with a smile attached to it! The unique value of this book is that you are sharing the ups and downs of the launch of a Unicorn, not just the glory of the fame, but also the doubts and challenges on the way. May it inspire you on your own journey to success and happiness.

THE RISE OF THE UNICORN 2 -076

eHappyPedia

BY Dr. BAK NGUYEN & Dr. JEAN DE SERRES

This is 2 years after starting the first tome. Dr. Bak's brand is picking up, between the accumulation of records and the recognition. eHappyPedia is now hot for a comeback. In THE RISE OF THE UNICORN 2, Dr. Bak is retracing and addressing each of Dr. Jean De Serres' concerns about the weakness of the first version of eHappyPedia and the eHappy movement. This is the sort of the creation and a UNICORN both in finance and in psychology. Never before, you will assist in such daily and decision-making process of a world phenomenon and of a company. Dr. Bak and Dr. De Serres are literally using the process of writing this series of books to plan and to brainstorm the birth of a bluechip. More than an intriguing story, this is the journey of 2 experienced entrepreneurs changing the world.

THE U.A.X STORY -072

THE ULTIMATE AUDIO EXPERIENCE

BY Dr. BAK NGUYEN

This is the story of the ULTIMATE AUDIO EXPERIENCE, U.A.X. Follow Dr. Bak's footstep on how he invented a new way to read and to learn. Dr. Bak brings his experience as a movie producer and a director to elevate the reading experience to another level with entertaining value and make it accessible to everyone, auditive, and visual people alike.

Three years plus of research and development, countless hours of trials and errors, Dr. Bak finally solved his puzzle: having written more than 1.1 million words. The irony is that he does not like to read, he likes audiobooks! U.A.X. finally allowed the opening of Dr. Bak's entire library to a new genre and media. U.A.X. is the new way to learn and enjoy Audiobooks. Made to be entertaining while keeping the self-educational value of a book, U.A.X. will appeal to both auditive and visual people. U.A.X. is the blockbuster of the Audiobooks. The format has already been approved by iTunes, Amazon, Spotify, and all major platforms for global distribution and streaming.

THE VACCINE -077

BY Dr. BAK NGUYEN & WILLIAM BAK

In THE VACCINE, A TALE OF SPIES AND ALIENS, Dr. Bak reprise his role as mentor to William, his 10 years-old son, both as co-author and as doctor. William is living through the COVID war and has accumulated many, many questions. That morning, they got out all at once. From a conversation between father and son, Dr. Bak is making science into words keeping the interest of his son a Saturday morning in bed. William is not just an audience, he is responsible to map the field with his questions. What started as a morning conversation between father and son, became within the next hour, a great project, their 23rd book together. Learn about the virus, vaccination while entertaining your kids.

TO OVERACHIEVE EVERYTHING BEING LAZY -090

CHEAT YOUR WAY TO SUCCESS

BY Dr. BAK NGUYEN

In TO OVERACHIEVE EVERYTHING BEING LAZY, Dr. Bak retaking his role talking to the millennials, the next generation. If in the first tome of the series LAZY, Dr. Bak addresses the general audience of millennials, especially young women, he is dedicating this tome to the ALPHA amongst the millennials, those aiming for the moon and looking, not only to be happy but to change the world. This is not another take on how to cheat your way to success or how to leverage laziness, but this is the recipe to build overachievers and rainmakers. For the young leaders with ambitions and talent, understanding TIME and ENERGY are crucial from your first steps writing your our legend. If Dr. Bak had the chance to do it all over again, this is how he would do it! Welcome to the Alphas.

TORNADO -067

FORCE OF CHANGE

BY Dr. BAK NGUYEN

In TORNADO - FORCE OF CHANGE Dr. Bak is writing solo. In the midst of the COVID war, change is not a good intention anymore. Change, constant change has become a new reality, a new norm. From somebody who holds the title of Industries' Disruptor, how does he yield change to stay in control? Well, the changes from the COVID war are constant fear and much loss of individual liberty. Some can endure the change, some will ride it. Dr. Bak is sharing his angle of navigating the changes, yielding the improvisations, and to reinvent the goals, the means to stay relevant. From fighting to keep his companies Dr. Bak went on to let go the uncontrollable to embrace the opportunity, he reinvented himself to ride the change and create opportunities from an unprecedented crisis. This is the story of a man refusing to kneel and accept defeat, smiling back at faith to find leverage and hope.

TOUCHSTONE -073

LEVERAGING TODAY'S PSYCHOLOGICAL SMOG

BY Dr. BAK NGUYEN & Dr. KEN SEROTA

TOUCHSTONE, LEVERAGING TODAY'S PSYCHOLOGICAL SMOG is mapping to navigate and to thrive in today's high and constant stress environment. After 40 years in practice, Dr. Serota is concerned about the evolution of the career of health care professionals and the never-ending level of stress. What is stress, what are its effects, damages, and symptoms? If COVID-19 revealed to the world that we are fragile, it also revealed most of the broken and the flaws of our system. For now a century, dentistry has been a champion in depression, Dr.ug addiction, and suicide rate, and the curve is far from flattening. Dr. Bak is sharing his perspective and experience dealing with stress and how to leverage it into a constructive force. From the stress of a doctor with no right to failure to the stress of an entrepreneur never knowing the future, Dr. Bak is sharing his way to use stress as leverage.

From Canada, **Dr BAK NGUYEN**, Nominee Ernst and Young Entrepreneur of the year, Grand Homage Lys DIVERSITY, and LinkedIn & TownHall Achiever of the year. Dr Bak is a cosmetic dentist, CEO and founder of Mdex & Co. His company is revolutionizing the dental field. Speaker and motivator, he wrote 72 books over 36 months accumulating many world records (to be officialized).

- **ENTREPRENEURSHIP**
- **LEADERSHIP**
- **QUEST OF IDENTITY**
- **DENTISTRY AND MEDICINE**
- **PARENTING**
- **CHILDREN BOOKS**
- **PHILOSOPHY**

In 2003, he founded Mdex, a dental company upon which in 2018, he launched the most ambitious private endeavour to reform the dental industry, Canada wide. Philosopher, he has close to his heart the quest of happiness of the people surrounding him, patients and colleagues alike. In 2020, he launched an International collaborative initiative named **THE ALPHAS** to share knowledge and for Entrepreneurs and Doctors to thrive through the Greatest Pandemic and Economic depression of our time.

In 2016, he co-found with Tranie Vo, Emotive World Incorporated, a tech research company to use technology to empower happiness and sharing. U.A.X. the ultimate audio experience is the landmark project on which the team is advancing, utilizing the technics of the movie industry and the advancement in ARTIFICIAL INTELLIGENCE to save the book industry and to upgrade the continuing education space.

These projects have allowed Dr Nguyen to attract interests from the international and diplomatic community and he is now the center of a global discussion in the wellbeing and the future of the health profession. It is in that matter that he shares his thoughts and encourages the health community to share their own stories.

"It's not worth it go through it alone! Together, we stand, alone, we fall."

Motivational speaker and serial entrepreneur, philosopher and author, from his own words, Dr Nguyen describes himself as a dentist by circumstances, an entrepreneur by nature and a communicator by passion.

He also holds recognitions from the Canadian Parliament and the Canadian Senate.

www.DrBakNguyen.com

AMAZON - BARNES & NOBLE - APPLE BOOKS - KINDLE
SPOTIFY - APPLE MUSIC

ULTIMATE AUDIO EXPERIENCE

A new way to learn and enjoy Audiobooks. Made to be entertaining while keeping the self-educational value of a book, UAX will appeal to both auditive and visual people. UAX is the blockbuster of the Audiobooks.

UAX will cover most of Dr Bak's books, and is now negotiating to bring more authors and more titles to the UAX concept. Now streaming on Spotify, Apple Music and available for download on all major music platforms. Give it a try today!

AMAZON - BARNES & NOBLE - APPLE BOOKS - KINDLE
SPOTIFY - APPLE MUSIC

FROM THE SAME AUTHOR

Dr Bak Nguyen

www.DrBakNguyen.com

MAJOR LEAGUES' ACCESS

FACTEUR HUMAIN -035
LE LEADERSHIP DU SUCCÈS
par Dr. BAK NGUYEN & CHRISTIAN TRUDEAU

THE RISE OF THE UNICORN -038
BY Dr. BAK NGUYEN & Dr. JEAN DE SERRES

CHAMPION MINDSET -039
LEARNING TO WIN
BY Dr. BAK NGUYEN & CHRISTOPHE MULUMBA

THE RISE OF THE UNICORN 2 -076
eHappyPedia
BY Dr. BAK NGUYEN & Dr. JEAN DE SERRES

BRANDING -044
BALANCING STRATEGY AND EMOTIONS
BY Dr. BAK NGUYEN

BUSINESS

SYMPHONY OF SKILLS -001
BY Dr. BAK NGUYEN

002 - **La Symphonie des Sens**
ENTREPREUNARIAT
par Dr. BAK NGUYEN

006 - **INDUSTRIES DISRUPTORS**
BY Dr .BAK NGUYEN

007 - **Changing the World from a dental chair**
BY Dr. BAK NGUYEN

008 - **The Power Behind the Alpha**
BY TRANIE VO & Dr. BAK NGUYEN

036 - **SELFMADE**
GRATITUDE AND HUMILITY
BY Dr. BAK NGUYEN

072 - **THE U.A.X. STORY**
THE ULTIMATE AUDIO EXPERIENCE
BY Dr. BAK NGUYEN

088 - **CRYPTOCONOMICS 101**
MY PERSONAL JOURNEY
FROM 50K TO 1 MILLION
BY Dr BAK NGUYEN

CHILDREN'S BOOK

with William Bak

The Trilogy of Legends

THE LEGEND OF THE CHICKEN HEART -016
LA LÉGENDE DU COEUR DE POULET -017
BY Dr. BAK NGUYEN & WILLIAM BAK

THE LEGEND OF THE LION HEART -018
LA LÉGENDE DU COEUR DE LION -019
BY Dr. BAK NGUYEN & WILLIAM BAK

THE LEGEND OF THE DRAGON HEART -020
LA LÉGENDE DU COEUR DE DRAGON -021
BY Dr. BAK NGUYEN & WILLIAM BAK

WE ARE ALL DRAGONS -022
NOUS TOUS, DRAGONS -023
BY Dr. BAK NGUYEN & WILLIAM BAK

THE 9 SECRETS OF THE SMART CHICKEN -025
LES 9 SECRETS DU POULET INTELLIGENT -026
BY Dr. BAK NGUYEN & WILLIAM BAK

THE SECRET OF THE FAST CHICKEN -027
LE SECRETS DU POULET RAPIDE -028
BY Dr. BAK NGUYEN & WILLIAM BAK

THE LEGEND OF THE SUPER CHICKEN -029
LA LÉGENDE DU SUPER POULET -030
BY Dr. BAK NGUYEN & WILLIAM BAK

031- **THE STORY OF THE CHICKEN SHIT**
032- **L'HISTOIRE DU CACA DE POULET**
BY Dr. BAK NGUYEN & WILLIAM BAK

033- **WHY CHICKEN CAN'T DREAM?**
034- **POURQUOI LES POULETS NE RÊVENT PAS?**
BY Dr. BAK NGUYEN & WILLIAM BAK

057- **THE STORY OF THE CHICKEN NUGGET**
083- **HISTOIRE DE POULET: LA PÉPITE**
BY Dr. BAK NGUYEN & WILLIAM BAK

082- **CHICKEN FOREVER**
084- **POULET POUR TOUJOURS**
BY Dr BAK NGUYEN & WILLIAM BAK

THE SPIES AND ALIENS COLLECTION

077- **THE VACCINE**
079- **LE VACCIN**
077B- **LA VACUNA**
BY Dr BAK NGUYEN & WILLIAM BAK
TRANSLATION BY BRENDA GARCIA

DENTISTRY

QUEST OF IDENTITY

LIFESTYLE

PERSONAL GROWTH

REBOOT -012
MIDLIFE CRISIS
BY Dr. BAK NGUYEN

HUMILITY FOR SUCCESS -051
BALANCING STRATEGY AND EMOTIONS
BY Dr. BAK NGUYEN

THE ENERGY FORMULA -053
BY Dr. BAK NGUYEN

AMONGST THE ALPHA -058
BY Dr. BAK NGUYEN & COACH JONAS DIOP

AMONGST THE ALPHA vol.2 -059
ON THE OTHER SIDE
BY Dr. BAK NGUYEN & COACH JONAS DIOP

THE 90 DAYS CHALLENGE -061
BY Dr. BAK NGUYEN

EMPOWERMENT -069
BY Dr BAK NGUYEN

THE MODERN WOMAN -070
TO HAVE IT HAVE WITH NO SACRIFICE
BY Dr. BAK NGUYEN & Dr. EMILY LETRAN

ALPHA LADDERS -075
CAPTAIN OF YOUR DESTINY
BY Dr BAK NGUYEN & JONAS DIOP

080- **1SELF**
REINVENT YOURSELF
FROM ANY CRISIS
BY Dr BAK NGUYEN

THE LAZY FRANCHISE

089- **THE CONFESSION OF A LAZY OVERACHIEVER**
BY Dr BAK NGUYEN

090- **TO OVERACHIEVE EVERYTHING BEING LAZY**
CHEAT YOUR WAY TO SUCCESS
BY Dr BAK NGUYEN

PHILOSOPHY

003- **LEADERSHIP** -003
PANDORA'S BOX
BY Dr. BAK NGUYEN

015- **FORCES OF NATURE**
FORGING THE CHARACTER
OF WINNERS
BY Dr BAK NGUYEN

040- **KRYPTO**
TO SAVE THE WORLD
BY Dr. BAK NGUYEN & ILYAS BAKOUCH

ALPHA LADDERS 2 -081
SHAPING LEADERS AND ACHIEVERS
BY Dr BAK NGUYEN & BRENDA GARCIA

MIRROR -085
BY Dr BAK NGUYEN

SHORTCUT

408 HEALING QUOTES -093
SHORTCUT VOLUME ONE
BY Dr. BAK NGUYEN

408 GROWTH QUOTES -094
SHORTCUT VOLUME TWO
BY Dr. BAK NGUYEN

365 LEADERSHIP QUOTES -095
SHORTCUT VOLUME THREE
BY Dr. BAK NGUYEN

518 CONFIDENCE QUOTES -096
SHORTCUT VOLUME FOUR
BY Dr. BAK NGUYEN

317 SUCCESS QUOTES -097
SHORTCUT VOLUME FIVE
BY Dr. BAK NGUYEN

376 POWER QUOTES -098
SHORTCUT VOLUME SIX
BY Dr. BAK NGUYEN

099- **306 HAPPINESS QUOTES**
SHORTCUT VOLUME SEVEN
BY Dr. BAK NGUYEN

100 - **170 DOCTOR QUOTES**
SHORTCUT VOLUME EIGHT
BY Dr. BAK NGUYEN

SOCIETY

013 - **LE RÊVE CANADIEN**
D'IMMIGRANT À MILLIONNAIRE
par DR BAK NGUYEN

054 - **CHOC**
LE JARDIN D'EDITH
par DR BAK NGUYEN

063 - **AFTERMATH**
BUSINESS AFTER THE GREAT PAUSE
BY Dr BAK NGUYEN & Dr ERIC LACOSTE

073 - **TOUCHSTONE**
LEVERAGING TODAY'S
PSYCHOLOGICAL SMOG
BY Dr BAK NGUYEN & Dr KEN SEROTA

074 - **COVIDCONOMICS**
THE GENERATION AHEAD
BY Dr BAK NGUYEN

THE POWER OF YES - 010
VOLUME ONE: IMPACT
BY Dr BAK NGUYEN

THE POWER OF YES 2 - 037
VOLUME TWO: SHAPELESS
BY Dr BAK NGUYEN

046 - **THE POWER OF YES 3**
VOLUME THREE: LIMITLESS
BY Dr BAK NGUYEN

087 - **THE POWER OF YES 4**
VOLUME FOUR: PURPOSE
BY Dr BAK NGUYEN

091 - **THE POWER OF YES 5**
VOLUME FIVE: ALPHA
BY Dr BAK NGUYEN

092 - **THE POWER OF YES 6**
VOLUME SIX: PERSPECTIVE
BY Dr BAK NGUYEN

www.DrBakNguyen.com

AMAZON - BARNES & NOBLE - APPLE BOOKS - KINDLE
SPOTIFY - APPLE MUSIC

DR.
Bak Nguyen

www.ingramcontent.com/pod-product-compliance
Lightning Source LLC
La Vergne TN
LVHW020712110826
845149LV00012B/2231

* 9 7 8 1 9 8 9 5 3 6 7 6 6 *